WALKING
and
RAMBLING

To all those writers, known and unknown, whose words I have quoted and whose information I have used.

To friends and relatives who have encouraged me, made useful suggestions and given me ideas.

To RLM and MDE for casting a critical and eagle eye on my rough scripts, for checking my interpretation of the legal situation and for causing me to rethink.

Heather MacDermid

WALKING
— *and* —
RAMBLING

Heather MacDermid

Hodder & Stoughton
LONDON SYDNEY AUCKLAND

TO MDE
The Complete Country Walking Companion
(provided there are no cows en route!)

The first colour map extract and legend, between pages 32 and 33, is from the 1987 Ordnance Survey 1:50 000 Landranger Series, Kettering, Corby & surrounding area map; and the second is from the 1987 Ordnance Survey 1:25 000 Pathfinder 895, Leicester (East) & Houghton on the Hill map. The extract on page 12 is from the Ordnance Survey 1:10 000 Tugby SK70SE map, and the extract on page 43 is from the Ordnance Survey 1:50 000 Landranger Series, Nottingham and Loughborough map (no 129). All are reproduced with the permission of the Controller of Her Majesty's Stationery Office © Crown Copyright.

Our thanks to the Dalesman Publishing Company Ltd. for their permission to reproduce the map on page 9 from *Walks in Lower Wharfedale*.

British Library Cataloguing in Publication Data

MacDermid, Heather
Teach yourself walking and rambling.
I. Title
796.5

ISBN 0 340 56779 1

First published 1992

Typeset by Rowland Phototypesetting Ltd,
Bury St Edmunds, Suffolk
Printed in Great Britain for the educational publishing division of Hodder & Stoughton Ltd, Mill Road, Dunton Green, Sevenoaks, Kent by Clays Ltd, St Ives plc, Bungay, Suffolk

CONTENTS

— INTRODUCTION —

Ask any ten walkers what is their main pleasure in walking and you are likely to be given more than ten different answers.

Most walkers mention the health-promoting qualities. Some view it as a kind of health and beauty class, with fresh air instead of music—they hope the exercise will help them keep fit and possibly slim. Many people regard walking as a therapeutic activity: a relaxation from the troubles of the world and of work; an escape into quiet and peaceful countryside.

Some obviously love the sense of adventure and challenge: the joy of exploring a route they have never trodden before, and of finding out what is over the next hill. For such romantic notions many a field is trodden.

More prosaically, many people choose walking as a cheap sport. Here is a form of exercise that is less expensive than Weight Watchers or aerobics classes. You need no special equipment: no bike or clubs, bowls, canoe or yacht. You have as much fresh air and a lot more scenery than golf, archery, or tennis. It is not a competitive sport: you do not need a partner, an opponent or a team; you do not need a coach or a cheer leader. And you can do it whatever your age or abilities. With a little ingenuity it is possible to select walks suitable for small children, pushchairs or wheelchairs, as well as routes that challenge and exhaust the most active teenagers and young adults.

When you walk you see the countryside much better than when you travel by car, and it's more economical and less stressful. As Dorothy Wordsworth wrote when she defended her eccentric choice of travelling on foot:

> My walking not only procured me infinitely more pleasure than I should have received from sitting in a post chaise but was also the means of saving me at least thirty shillings.
>
> (From a letter written to Mrs Christopher Cracken Thorpe, 21 April 1794.)

Your interests may, of course, be purely utilitarian. You may be a food-for-free devotee, noting every crop of elderflower and berry, every sloe and dandelion for wine-making, crab apples for jam, rosehips for syrup, mushrooms for breakfast, and each bed of nettles or sorrel for tea, soup or salads.

Among any group of walkers there are photographers, framing the views and focussing on the detail around them, or artists looking for scenes to sketch. There may be dedicated students of deserted medieval villages, of industrial archeology or natural history and farming practice, as well as railway fanatics, recognising with glee the lines they rode in their youth.

Some walkers set out to explore towpaths, or Roman roads, or Sites of Scientific Interest. There are devotees of old drove roads, saltways, packhorse bridges, lime kilns, lock gates, sheep pens, drystone walls, cruck cottages, brick patterning, weather vanes and a host of other items which can be seen on a normal day's walking.

The country walker may never be able to encompass them all, but can learn to look and listen and appreciate the fascination they hold for the enthusiast—and wait while the photograph is taken, or the sketch drawn, or the notes scribbled down. The enthusiasm, after all, may be catching. And if you do want to develop your interest there are books in the library on every imaginable topic!

Why read this book?

This book is written to encourage people who want to walk on footpaths and tracks in the country. It aims to answer those questions that interest, worry or intrigue walkers, and to give practical advice about equipment. It is not intended for hill walkers and mountain climbers: they are referred to more advanced technical books.

Newcomers to country walking often find it difficult to know where to go, how to start, how to find the track, how to ensure it is a legal right of way and how to find out if it is safe.

Many people who have tried following a footpath sign that pointed enticingly into open countryside have been disappointed to find themselves in an open field with no way of knowing which way to go next. Some have walked with a map or guide book in their hand and found the route barred by impenetrable hedges or barbed wire or ploughed land and high crops. Others have been frightened by large animals and have decided never to leave the road again, preferring the dangers of the motor vehicle to the uncertainty of the fields.

But the joys and delights of walking in the countryside are still to be found. Country walking is, in fact, one of the most popular outdoor sports. For those who walk with a group there is the added bonus of good companionship and the chance to learn from others something about plants, birds, animals, rocks, farming practice or signs of history on the ground. Those who walk alone have the pleasure of going at their own pace in their own choice of country, pausing in their own time to admire the views and to explore the things that interest them.

Whether you walk alone or lead others, you need to be able to find a route, to check that it is a right of way, to know your legal rights and responsibilities, and to be aware of changes in the countryside that might affect your walking. This book aims to address those issues, to give guidance about sensible clothing and equipment, and to help people walk with confidence in the countryside.

In my own long love affair with footpaths, I have worn out many a pair of boots, bought many an Ordnance Survey map and guide book, and found great delight in exploring the countryside, both on my own and with friends. I have had my eyes opened and my spirit refreshed by the beauty and quiet of areas not yet spoilt by the pressures of urban development.

I hope that this book will help you to enjoy your country walking.

Heather MacDermid

1

PREPARING TO WALK

There is a marvellous variety of walking countryside within a small space in Britain. Even if we exclude the wilder regions of moorland and mountain and leave them to books for the experienced walker, there are still many different kinds of walks to choose from.

You may decide you are a 'flat land' walker, preferring to keep to river valleys and fen country. You may, on the other hand, want a challenge that stretches your legs. Perhaps you want to be near the sea, with the ups and downs of coastal paths; or perhaps you want to try one of the named long distance paths, such as Offa's Dyke or the Cleveland Way (see Chapter 7). You could try the mixed scenery of a particular part of the country that has been recommended by friends, or that you have read about or seen on TV and always wanted to visit.

You may feel you want to explore nearer home: and it is certainly amazing to discover what lovely paths there are on one's own doorstep. A few miles outside most cities there is a treasure-house of beautiful unspoilt countryside.

If you are lucky enough to live on the edge of town you may be able to walk straight from your house out across fields—and yet perhaps you never have done so. Perhaps you have been out at work all day, busy in the evenings and off in the car at weekends. You may not have known there were footpaths across those fields. Now is the time to look at your local maps and explore.

You might find you can get on a local bus and return the same evening after a good full day's walking in lovely scenery which you have sped past a hundred times in the car, bus or the train and never realised it was possible to walk there. By using the countryside around you, you can get yourself into training for long holiday walks and practise your map reading skills.

However you walk, wherever you go, whoever you walk with, and whatever your interests, your walks will be enhanced by knowledge of the area and confidence in your map-reading.

1.1 Route planning

For any walking, deciding where you want to go can be done with a good big road map. You can choose the area you want to walk in by:

- Measuring a certain distance from home and deciding to keep within so many miles' travelling to get there;
- Looking at the map and choosing an area that looks attractive because it is near the sea, or the woods, or the hills or the canal, or a lot of old castles . . . ;
- Choosing an area for personal reasons of your own;
- Or by closing your eyes and sticking a pin in the map.

Wherever you choose, you will need to work out how to get there and back, checking whether it is best to use car, public transport, friends, relatives, taxi . . . ?

You can use the same method for choosing walks for a day out or for a week's holiday walking, or even if you are making a year's programme for a club or a group of friends. First choose your area, and then work out how you are going to travel there and back.

Libraries, bookshops and tourist information centres can help you find out what there is to see and do in the area of your choice. Local guide books often recommend particular walks, and booklets, pamphlets and leaflets are available to direct you along little-known paths to interesting places you might never have discovered yourself.

After Christmas, when the TV adverts are persuading you to book holidays, and showing lots of other people diving into pools or lying soaking up the sun, you could decide to escape from the crowds by walking in quiet places. I browse through my copies of country walking magazines, or I go to the library for books about Yorkshire, or Wales or the Isle of Mull . . . or wherever my feet fancy. Then I write to the relevant tourist board for details of walks and places to visit. Once I have an idea of what there is to do, I plan where to walk and what to stop and see (little markets and museums, castles and caves), and what to do in the evenings or on dreary wet days.

For accommodation, I start to look for possible places to stay in *Where to Stay—Bed and Breakfast Farmhouses, Inns and Hotels,* published by the English Tourist Board; or *Staying Off the Beaten Track* by Elizabeth Gundry, published by Arrow. Or I ask friends if they can recommend a farm or guest house.

You may decide not to go away for a holiday this year, but to try instead walking every path in your district, or every walk in the local footpath guide book, or the nearest long distance route. You can work out how to return home each night and how to organise transport to the start and finish of each day out. You may find, as I do, that every walk will be as good as a holiday, and that you come back feeling refreshed and relaxed.

1.2 Maps

Ordnance Survey Pathfinder and Landranger maps are a walker's best friends. There are examples of both between pages 32 and 33.

Landranger maps give a good overview of an area. The scale of these maps is what I still call one inch to the mile, though they have long since been decimalised to 1:50000 (ie. 1cm to 0.5km). You can measure a mile very roughly with your thumbnail, or the top joint of your thumb.

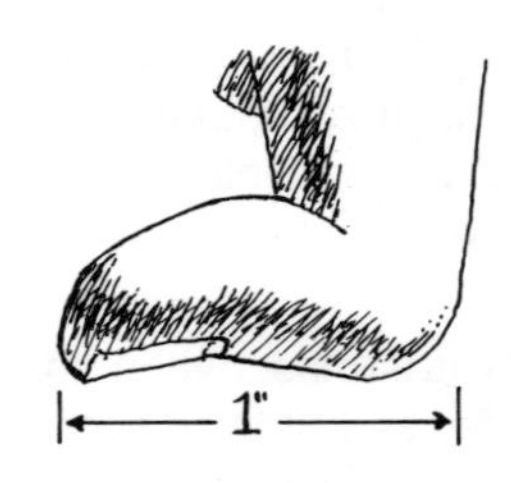

The maps are colourful and clear and help you find an area that looks attractive for walking, and the roads you are going to need for travelling there and back.

The guide sheet at the edge shows you the symbols used for roads and paths. Footpaths are marked in red dots, bridleways in red dashes.

Tourist information includes car parking areas, picnic places, good viewpoints and camp sites.

Clearly marked are rivers and streams, marshes and lakes, railways (used and disused), quarries, woods, windmills, post offices, pubs, public toilets and telephones.

Pathfinder maps cover a smaller area, but in much more detail. The scale is 1:25000, or 4cms to 1km. (Old style, two and a half inches to a mile.) You can measure a mile very roughly with your whole thumb.

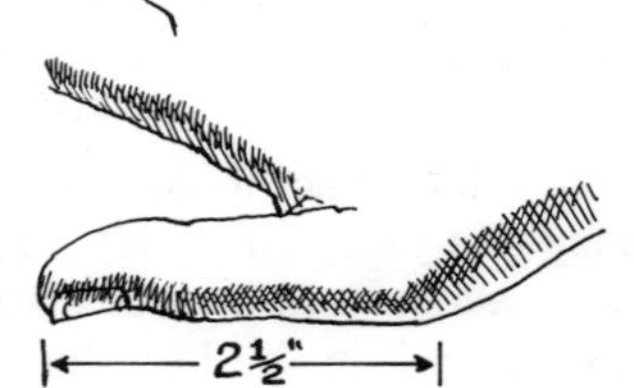

These maps have footpaths and bridleways marked in green, and each hedge is finely drawn in black. Again, streams, lakes, churches, mills and woods are all marked and the back cover explains all the symbols.

A **1:10000** (6 inch) **map** has no colouring and is not much use in the field as you so quickly walk off the edge. It indicates every building and can pinpoint more accurately where a path runs. It is very useful for legal matters over disputed paths because it gives the footpath number of every path.

Simplified maps in guide books (like the well-known ones by Wainwright) give a line drawing of one path only. These are meant to make life easier for you and it is certainly less difficult to keep your place on a guide book map than on an OS sheet when you are struggling in a high wind with conversation, children, binoculars, camera, picnic food and drink, dog on lead, history book, bird book, flower and tree manuals.

The disadvantage is that you have no choice of alternative paths and, if you do deviate from the author's chosen route, you have no way of finding a different way back.

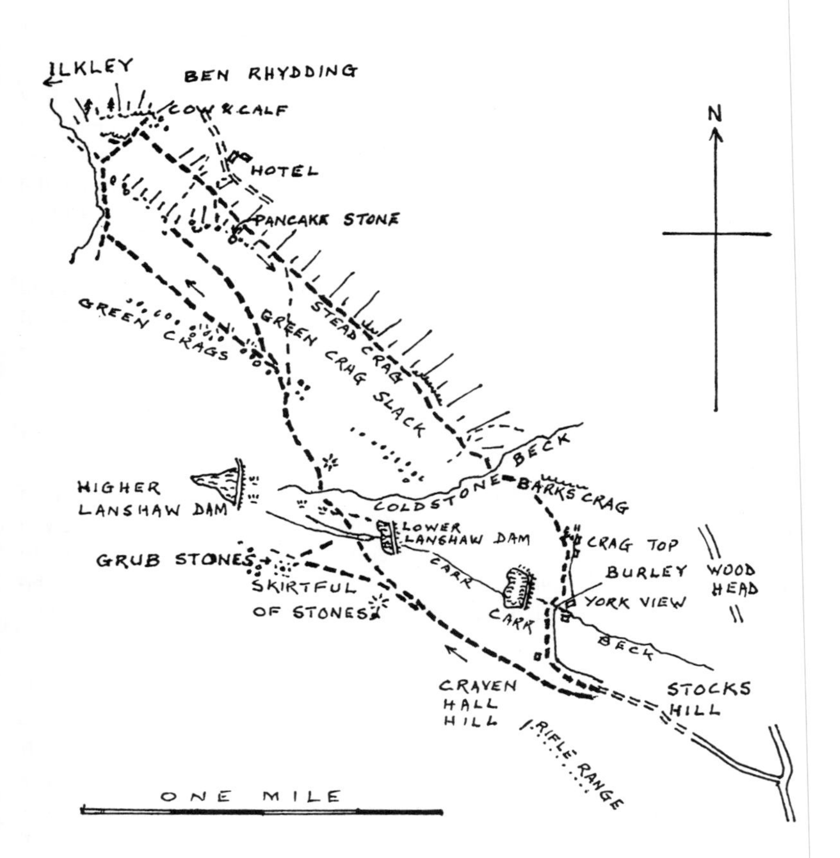

Using maps

The following examples give an idea of the advantages of the different maps. I personally follow a 'belt and braces' rule and often take several kinds of map with me. A cross-check can be revealing.

Imagine a walk from and around Tugby.

The 1:50000 **Landranger map** (between pages 32 and 33) shows that the main A47 road goes close to the village of Tugby. You can see where the church is, and reckon that you will be able to park your car somewhere near it. Or you will check whether you can get there by bus or train. You can see there is a pub, and there is a telephone box that might be useful if you want to contact home.

There is a useful-looking triangle of red dotted paths. Measure roughly with your thumb knuckle. It looks about 3 or 4 miles. That might be fine to begin with. If you are a fast walker you could do it in a couple of hours, including a tour of the village and a look in the church. You could go in a leisurely fashion and admire the views, taking a whole morning with lunch at the pub.

The path starts from the main road and goes diagonally downhill, as you can see from the brown contour lines. (Contour lines show the height of the ground above sea level. When they appear close together, this indicates a steep slope. More widely-spaced lines indicate a gentle slope.) The path crosses a stream at the bottom of the hill, goes past a wood and uphill to the top corner of another little wood. It then turns left along a line of red dashes. (It has changed from a footpath to a bridleway, which means it might be a wider and better path, with gates instead of stiles.) It goes absolutely straight until it meets a minor road. You will need to turn right for a short distance along the road and then turn left, to continue in the same direction as the last section of the path. (Will the bridleway be signposted? It should be, as this is where it joins a highway road.)

The path should go straight towards a Works building on the main road. (The map does not show what sort of Works. Perhaps that will become clear as you get nearer to it.) At the main road, you will need to turn left and walk along the busy A47 for a short distance. The next footpath will be on your right and should be signposted. It looks as if it goes slightly downhill (according to the contours), so you might be able to see the church tower. (The square base of the church symbol shows it's a tower and not a spire.) You have to go through part of the village before you reach the church. Perhaps the way through will be signposted.

The area looks pleasantly wooded and gently undulating with views down over a river valley and out to hills beyond. Robin-a-Tiptoe looks an interesting name and Whatborough Hill has a trig point of 230, which is a bit higher than Robin-a-Tiptoe's 221. (Trig, or trigonometric, point is a spot on a hilltop that is used for measuring by a surveyor.)

The 1:25000 **Pathfinder map** (between pages 32 and 33) shows more clearly where the path begins (with green dots this time). It is about one hundred metres along the road, and it should be marked by a footpath sign. You need to cross a hedge (marked with a fine black line) into the corner of a second field (where three lines meet) and go down to the stream, keeping in the same direction. When you have crossed the stream the path goes slightly to the right, to the corner of the field. (There may be a waymark sign, to mark the route, and a stile.) From the bottom corner of the next field the path goes uphill to the top right-hand corner of the field near a wood. Then it turns left, along a bridleway (green dashes) with a hedge (fine black line) on the left all the way to the road. Then it turns right for a hundred yards or less along the road, then left, with a hedge on the left for most of the way.

You will have to check whether this continuous hedge ends unexpectedly, as they sometimes do. If it does you will have to look closely at the map to see whether you are in the last field before the road. It is a good idea to count hedge junctions as you pass them. Is Skeffington Gap farm just one field away in front of you? If so, you need to swing just slightly to the left to reach the road. Perhaps there will be a track through the crops to guide you, or perhaps you will be able to judge by the shape of the field and the hedge facing you.

Turn left along the main road and go into the second field on the right (is there a footpath sign?). There is no hedge to guide you here: the path goes diagonally across the field. You can see the general direction and aim to move away from the main road gradually. If there is a gate or an obvious stile, that will indicate the direction for the next two fields. There should be a crossing in the far corner of the last field, and then you walk with a hedge on your left through part of the village until you reach the church. Perhaps the way through will be marked.

If there are any problems you could look at the 1:10000 **Definitive map** (see p12).

You can see the numbers of the paths you took, so if you need to report an obstruction you can say it is on the B85, or the B81, or the B89. If you need to check whether you crossed that last field in the right place, you

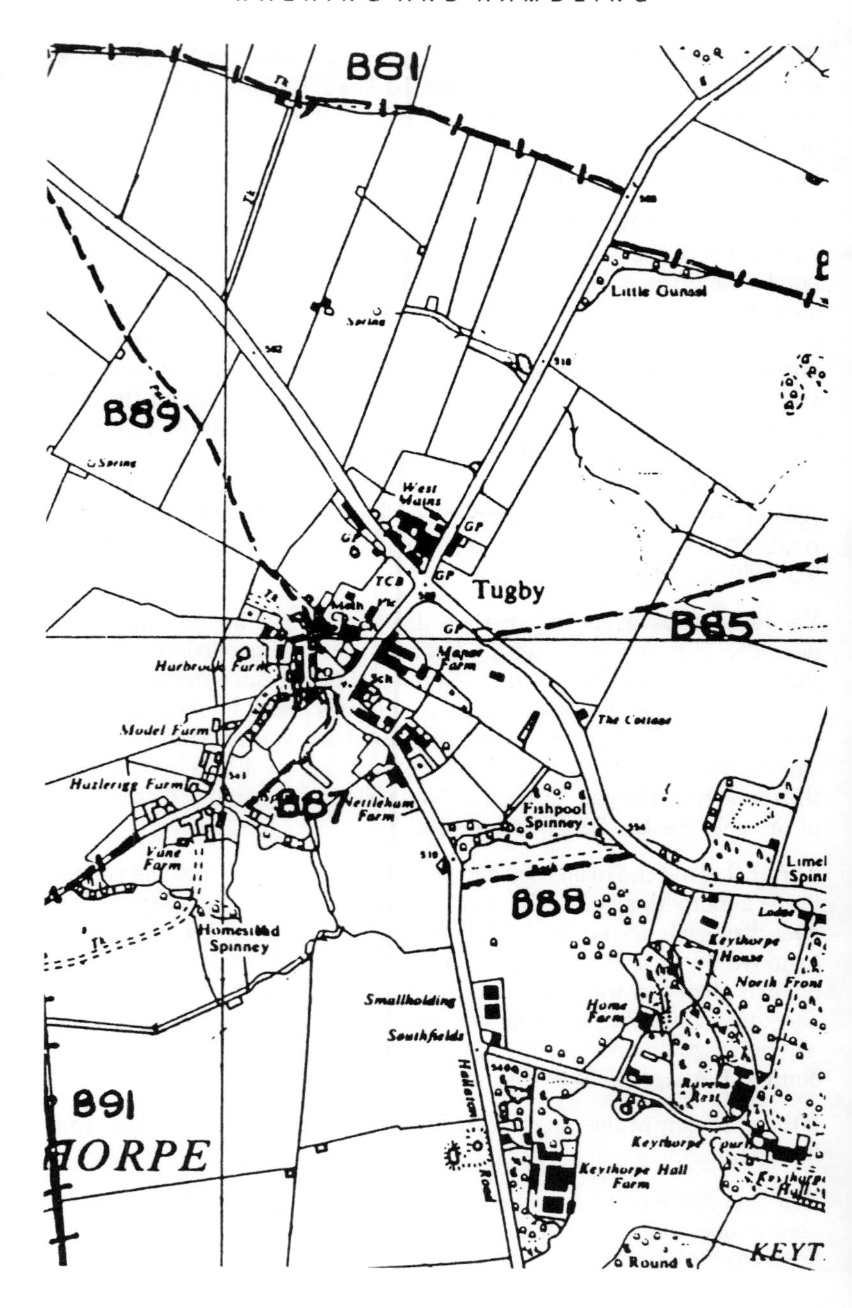

B81
Little Gunsel
B89
Spring
West Mains
GP
TCB
Tugby
B85
Manor Farm
The Cottage
Model Farm
Hazlerigg Farm
B87
Nettleham Farm
Fishpool Spinney
Vane Farm
B88
Homestead Spinney
Smallholding
Southfields
Keythorpe House
North Front
Home Farm
Ravens Rest
Keythorpe Court
Keythorpe Hall Farm
Hallaton Road
B91
ORPE
Round
KEYT

can look closely to see on which side of the hedge the path really is. The map shows some farms with interesting names. Perhaps this calls for a little walk around the village? The B87 path should bring you back to the church.

I love maps. They make me want to get out and explore! If I walk beyond the post office in the village, I take a map. You never know where it might lead you, or what you might discover.

1.3 Ground plans

When you have decided where you intend to go walking, you need to look closely at your map to see what sort of terrain there is going to be. Your 1:50 000 map will show you whether it is flat or hilly, and where the rivers and woods are. If there are a lot of contour lines close together then there will be steep hills.

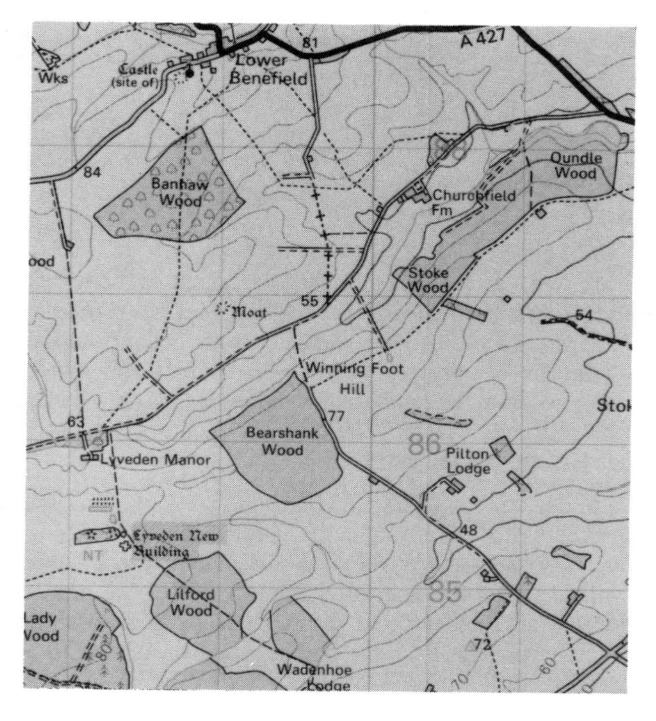

If it is a coastal path with lots of bays and inlets it quite probably has a lot of steep climbs down to the seashore and back up again (and the climbs down are often nearly as strenuous as the struggle back up again!)

If it is an area with a lot of fine black field lines round small enclosures you may discover you have many difficult stiles to cross.

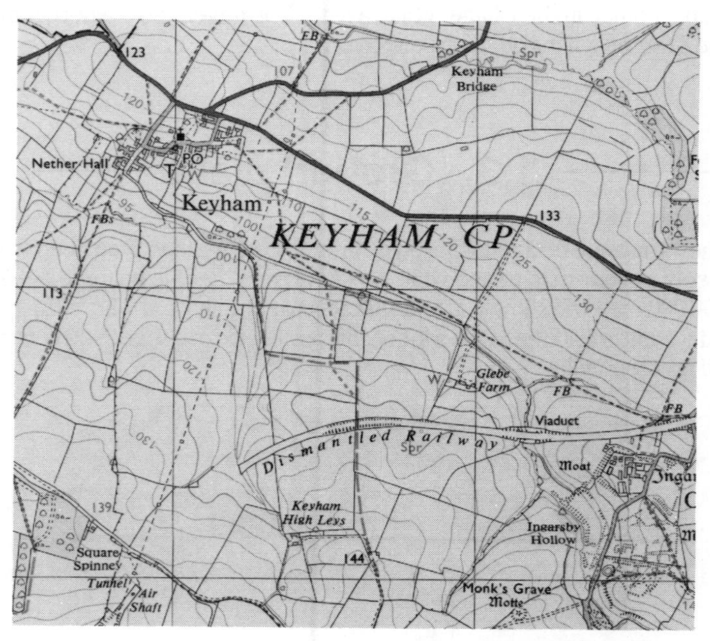

If there are woods, you may be lucky enough to find well laid-out woodland tracks: but you need to check that they are real paths leading through the wood and not just woodland trails going round and round inside it. (Beware of Forestry Commission tracks leading into the dead end working area for the lumberjacks. They are often temptingly wide and straight: but they will get you nowhere.) You will need a compass to check that you are not led astray.

You need to decide what distance you want to walk before you venture into unknown territory. Find out in the countryside nearest to your home what kind of distance suits you best, then decide how much extra time or energy you need for the special characteristics of the area you have chosen for walking further afield. You need to make allowance for mud, stiles, difficult crossings in arable farming country, hills, cliffs, bays and sandy foreshores.

1.4 Measuring distances

A guide book will usually tell you the distance of the walk described, and often it will give you an idea of the time required to complete it. If you are planning your own route, you can measure distances with a special map measuring wheel or make a rough estimate with your thumb.

For a more accurate measurement, you can make yourself a knotted measuring string by tying knots at intervals to coincide with the scale on the margin of your map. You can then lay this out along your intended route and the knots give you an instant measurement.

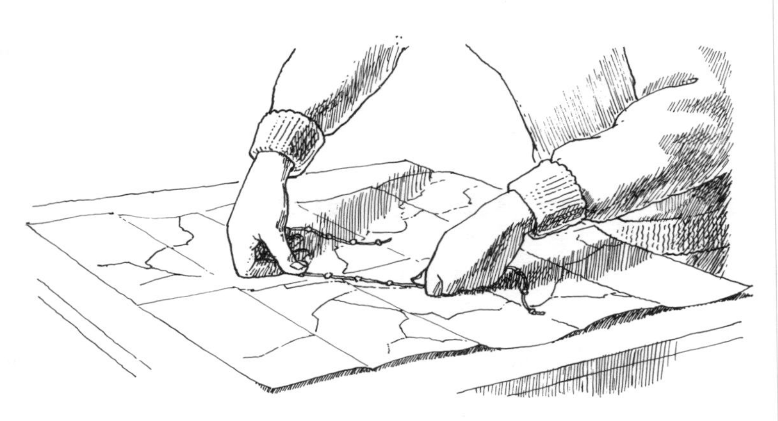

When you have decided how many miles you want to cover you can work out how long it will take you to walk that distance.

1.5 Estimating time

Most people find that an average walking speed works out over a whole day (including picnic stops) as:

4 miles per hour for road walking at a fairly fast speed
3 miles per hour on good flat tracks
2 miles per hour for field walking

For mountain climbing, hill walkers use Napier's rule about adding so many minutes for every contour line uphill. (John Napier was a Scottish mathematician who lived from 1550–1617 and invented all kinds of mathematical rules.) For country walking you need only accept the general principle that it is going to take a bit longer to walk up and down hills than to walk along lowland paths; and that each hedge, fence or boundary stile, every stream or ditch, and every ploughed field you have to cross, will slow you down.

It is useful to have a rough idea of the time you are likely to finish your walk, so that you can plan your transport home or your evening meal—or the time for your immersion heater or central heating time-switch to spring into action ready for your return. As a very rough estimate, allow four hours for an eight-mile walk and five hours for a ten-miler. Much depends, of course, on your general strength, agility and stamina (and the time you take to eat your picnics). So test yourself for your average speed.

But remember that country walking is not a race against time, it is meant to be a pleasure, as well as a means of keeping fit. Allow yourself as much time as you need . . . and a bit to spare for unexpected delays.

1.6 Weather

Red sky at night
Shepherd's delight

Fine weather following that pink/red evening sky makes for pleasant walking.

Red sky in the morning
Sailor's warning

But poor weather does not necessarily mean a poor walk.

For mountain and moorland walking good weather might be absolutely crucial for safety, but for normal country walking it is not so essential. You can have very enjoyable country walks in quite rough weather, without needing the assistance of any rescue team. You should, however, take sensible precautions for the variety of weather you are likely to encounter, and dress accordingly.

Many serious walkers ignore forecasts completely and set off prepared for any kind of weather. They may perhaps glance at a TV news bulletin or listen to a radio forecast for a general idea of the weather to come: but they won't necessarily believe that this will be at all accurate for the little pocket of land they are going to walk in.

You could consult the local paper's weather forecast, or phone the nearest weather station (under *Meteorological Office* in your telephone directory), but you may find your own memories of folklore weather-forecasting quite accurate enough for you to make the necessary adjustments to dress and equipment.

You could try looking at clouds:

When clouds appear like rocks and towers
The earth's refreshed by frequent showers.

Or noting the behaviour of bees:

If bees stay at home
Rain will come soon.
If they fly away
Fine will be the day.

I have one friend who will not set out on a walk if it is actually raining. While another swears by:

Rain before seven
Clear before eleven

and

A sunshiny shower
Won't last an hour.

The first friend misses many lovely walks: the second often ends up rather wet.

You can choose your own tactics for rain, depending on whether it is winter or summer, on whether you know the route or not, on how waterproof your clothes are, how delicate your constitution and how much you want to walk, and whether you can spare the time to wait for a drier day. You may positively enjoy walking in the wind and rain!

There are some points to bear in mind when deciding whether or not to go:

- Rain always slows you down if map reading is required: it takes much longer to get the map out of its plastic bag, wipe the raindrops off it, dry your hands and wipe your glasses. And if you decide not to check with the map, then it takes even longer if you get lost!
- You could go to the starting point, ready to set off at the first sign of clear sky. If you stay at home you may well miss an hour of good walking weather.
- When you are covered in waterproofs, rain does not always feel as bad as it looks from behind a window pane.
- A wet walk can be very enjoyable, especially when it's over!

> I had a very wet windy walk home (to Haworth) from Keighley but my fatigue quite disappeared when I reached home and found all well.
>
> Charlotte Brontë (Letter to Ellen Nussey dated 25 September 1847).

If you have set off in fine weather and realise that 'it looks a bit black over Bill's mother's', or notice that all the cows are sitting down, you might need to speed up to avoid oncoming rain.

If you are leading a group and you don't manage to speed up enough to avoid the coming rain, you can try cheering them up with such gems of folk wisdom as:

> It'll soon be over. There's enough blue in the sky to make a sailor a pair of trousers.

In Spring you can try:

> March winds and April showers
> Bring forth May flowers.

Rain, of course, can occur in every season and so can windy weather. This, too, might slow you down if the wind is against you, or because it causes map problems. But before you decide never to walk in the rain or the wind, read the section on equipment.

Summer is not necessarily the best time for walking. If you don't like hot weather, it would probably be wisest not to take your walking holiday during July and August. However, if you do choose summer walking, remember that heatwaves slow you down because you feel less energetic, and you stop more often for drinks and rests.

> Whan that Aprille with his shoures swete
> The droghte of March hath perced to the rote
> Than longen folke to go on pilgrimages.
> Geoffrey Chaucer *Prologue to the Canterbury Tales*

April is the month when most people fancy walking in the countryside, before the sun gets too hot or the crops grow too high—and when you can still see the church spire ahead of you through the flimsily-leaved trees. The fresh green tempts you out to mark the paths with your feet and steal a march on the summer.

Autumn, the 'Season of mists and mellow fruitfulness' (Keats *Ode to Autumn*), is as beautiful as summer, and it is easier to walk when the harvest is safely gathered in.

Winter walking is often very enjoyable, but the days are short and you must make the most of them. The skies are sometimes blue and a brisk walk can be very cheering. Cold weather usually speeds you up, in your desire to keep warm (and to get back home to the warm fire and hot chocolate).

Deep snow makes the way impossibly difficult, but if the path has been well trodden and beaten down by other feet, the covering of snow only slows you down. (But check that you have a good gripping sole on your wellies or boots to minimise the danger of slipping, and beware of being caught in further snowfalls.)

> Every month from the beginnings of life in the early spring through the full summer days with purple heather, gay as a garden, stretching further than the eye can reach, to the varied colourings of mid autumn, has delights and compensations of its own, which ought to send her back to the toil and moil of everyday life refreshed and as recreated.
>
> Lucretia Clark, c1880 *Hints for Holidays*
>
> (For the hundreds of women who can walk with benefit fifty to a hundred miles a week . . . who have not yet found it out.)

1.7 Escape routes

It is always a good idea to have an escape route plan, just in case you loitered too long over lunch or stopped too long chatting to the Oldest Inhabitant of the village—or for if the weather turns nasty or someone develops blisters or needs to get home early. Here are some ideas for contingency plans:

- Try and plan two routes, one long and one short, or one strenuous and one easy.
- Are there sections of your walk where you could choose a valley route instead of going over the tops? Or a lane as a less demanding substitute for the little field paths with awkward stiles?
- See if there is a way off your route to reach a main road.
- See if someone could meet you to transport you back if you rang up with a map reference.
- Get hold of bus time-tables and find out if there is a bus route.
- Make a note of the number of a local taxi service.
- Carry enough money for the phone call and for the fare. (Phone boxes are marked on OS maps with a large T, or a telephone symbol.)
- See if you can find a good place to wait and shelter until you are rescued.

1.8 Stopping places

You can either carry food with you or plan to eat at a pub or café along the way. If you take a picnic you can eat where and when you want, looking at the best view. If not, you can travel lighter—but it is still a good idea to take a snack along, just in case there is nowhere to buy food. It is a good idea to eat after, rather than before, you have climbed a hill: that way, you don't have to slog uphill on a full stomach. Here are some tips for an enjoyable picnic:

- Sit at the top of a hill where you can admire the view while you congratulate yourself.
- Sit on a waterproof, even if the ground seems dry.
- Protect yourself from cold winds on the top.
- If it rains find shelter, in a barn or behind a wall or hedge.
- If it thunders, avoid the highest trees.

Dress up for dinner if you are eating out! Put on an extra layer! You will feel the chill when you rest in the open air, even if you find a sheltered spot.

Pub lunches

If you are planning to eat at a pub, check beforehand when it is open and whether they serve food. If you are taking a group, it is a good idea to warn them in advance how many people there are likely to be. You can look up local pubs in the telephone book.

When you go into a pub, offer to remove or cover your boots. You can carry plastic bags to serve as slippers to protect your socks from wet or mucky pub floors, or as overshoes to protect expensive pub carpeting from your muddy boots!

There is nothing to beat the comfort of a roaring country pub fireside and a glass of ginger beer shandy or ginger wine before you tackle the next ten miles!

In reasonable weather you might be able to use the beer garden to eat your sandwiches—but do not expect to eat your own food inside the pub, or use the toilets without buying a drink

Tea rooms

Tea rooms are less numerous than pubs and they tend to be more elegant, so it is even more important to be considerate with your boots and haversack, particularly in popular tourist places.

Places of interest

It is a good idea to look upon your walk as your primary objective, with any other activities as optional extras. It is often more tiring to combine different activities, because you lose your walking rhythm. Touring round the castle walls may be the most exhausting part of your walk.

Of course the advantage of organising your own walk is that you can do and see just what you want, but it might be sensible to make some sort of rule to limit your stops en route. You *could* decide:

- Only one town per walk
- Only one castle, museum or craft fair a day
- Only the outside of any stately home or palace
- No stops until after the day's walk is done
- Separate your photography, your sketching, your wine harvesting, your caving, etc from your general walking days
- Plan shorter walks to accommodate more activities.

Stopping the night

Most walks can be done in a day. But if you are planning a longer walk, or doing several walks in one area, you are going to be happier knowing you have a bed and supper for the night. You can book in advance at a hotel, guest house, farmhouse or hotel. The advantage of this is that you do not have to spend time at the end of the day searching for accommodation—you might have to walk a considerable distance off your planned route before you find a suitable place.

There are tremendously good value farmhouses off the beaten track, and various magazines specialise in advertising them. Tourist information centres in country towns list names, addresses and telephone numbers of local people offering accommodation and will ring to book for you, at a small charge. Your own town's information centre can provide addresses and telephone numbers of all the other centres, so that you can acquire accommodation lists from any area you want to visit.

If you are ready for adventure and like the freedom of travelling without pre-booking you might prefer the last minute search for a place to lay your head at night. But if you have companions with you it would be better to check whether they, too, are happy to leave it to the last minute, or if they would find it more reassuring to know where they are to eat and sleep.

If you are really planning to immerse yourself in the great outdoors you might want to backpack and carry your tent and cooking equipment with you. You can look out for suitable places to camp as you go along, or find out in advance where there are good sites. Do bear in mind that you will need to carry a lot more weight. If you are backpacking for the first time it is probably a good idea to read a book about it, or join a club.

2

SETTING OFF

2.1 Clothes

One of the best things about country walking is that you don't really need much expensive equipment. Generations of people have walked in their daily outdoor working clothes. Wordsworth rambled the Lake District wearing his brother Richard's cast-off coats. Emily and Charlotte Brontë walked out on the moors around Haworth in their long heavy skirts, 'to the great damage of our shoes (but I hope, to the benefit of our health).' (Letter to Ellen Nussey dated 7 April 1844.)

For specialist walking clothes my favourite bit of advice comes from a lady (Lucretia Clark) writing to the *Daily Chronicle* in the early 1880s:

> What to wear on one's feet is the most important and difficult question of all . . . It is a mark of wisdom to keep our best fitting boots for walking tours . . . and boots are better than shoes. A long sleeved Jaeger combination, beige knickerbockers, jacket, skirt and underskirt and blouse will keep a healthy woman warm in summer and autumn . . . Choose good, all wool material which is not hurt by wetting. Avoid all colours which lose their dye . . . The underskirt does not require lining, and should be about ten inches shorter than the dress . . . For even if the dress clears the ground by four or five inches, it is a great help to slip it off and carry it over the shoulder when crossing the moors where one sinks well up to the knee among the heather . . . or if

> this cannot be done, the skirt can be shortened with strong safety pins. A soft felt hat and gloves are necessary for the villages . . .
>
> And what must be taken for the comfort of a week's walk? A leathern bag slung over the shoulder will hold a nightdress, extra combination, pair of knickerbockers and stockings, slippers, comb etc, carefully keeping down every ounce of weight. Anything beyond that is required can be sent to meet one at a given point.
>
> A strong stick is better than an umbrella, and there would be no pleasure in walking in a mackintosh, if it could be taken . . . Keep in motion till an inn can be reached and clothes dried. A brisk rub and a cup or two of some warm drink are preventives against taking cold. Indeed it is astonishing how seldom colds do occur in these cases.
>
> More of a necessity than a luxury are a map of the district and a book for the evenings and the midday lounge.
>
> A few sandwiches will carry a pedestrian ten or twenty miles to a good evening meal.

Our ideas about length of skirts and kinds of underwear may have changed, but we must admire her grasp of the priorities: comfortable footwear, windproof and waterproof outer gear, food and a bag over the shoulders to carry a minimum of extras to make yourself decent for public places.

Footwear

For your first walks, especially in dry weather, comfortable flat shoes with a strong, thick sole will be adequate. Some people never buy anything else. Everyone's feet are different—while some can withstand anything, others need nurturing. But if you are planning to walk regularly in all kinds of weather and over rough, stony ground, it is a good idea to protect your feet in special walking boots or shoes.

Whether you buy cheap or expensive boots is really a matter of taste. I've had expensive ones that leaked, or which were too heavy and stiff and caused blisters. Cheap foreign imports or working men's boots, or a market stall pair, often turn out to be perfectly adequate, although the cheap ones may not last quite so long as the expensive ones, nor stand up to such hard wear. Leather boots are best because they allow your feet to 'breathe'.

Rubber boots trap perspiration and condensation inside, so that your feet may become slightly damp and uncomfortable. Canvas boots have now

Landranger 1:50 000

ROADS AND PATHS

Not necessarily rights of way

Service area M 1

Elevated

Junction number 1

Motorway

Motorway under construction

Unfenced

Footbridge

A 6 (T)

Trunk road

Dual carriageway

A 50

Main road

Main road under construction

B 664

Secondary road

A 855

B 885

Narrow road with passing places

Bridge

Road generally more than 4 m wide

Road generally less than 4 m wide

Other road, drive or track

Path

PUBLIC RIGHTS OF WAY

(Not applicable to Scotland)

Footpath

Bridleway

Road used as a public path

Byway open to all traffic

GENERAL FEATURES

Electricity transmission line

Pipe line

ruin

Buildings

Public buildings (selected)

Bus or coach station

Coniferous wood

Non-coniferous wood

Mixed wood

Orchard

Park or ornamental grounds

Quarry

Spoil heap, refuse tip or dump

Radio or TV mast

Church or Chapel with tower

Church or Chapel with spire

Church or Chapel without tower or spire

Chimney or tower

Glasshouse

Graticule intersection at 5′ intervals

Heliport

Triangulation pillar

Windmill with or without sails

Windpump

ABBREVIATIONS

P	Post office
PH	Public house
MS	Milestone
MP	Milepost
CH	Clubhouse
PC	Public convenience (in rural areas)
TH	Town Hall, Guildhall or equivalent
CG	Coastguard

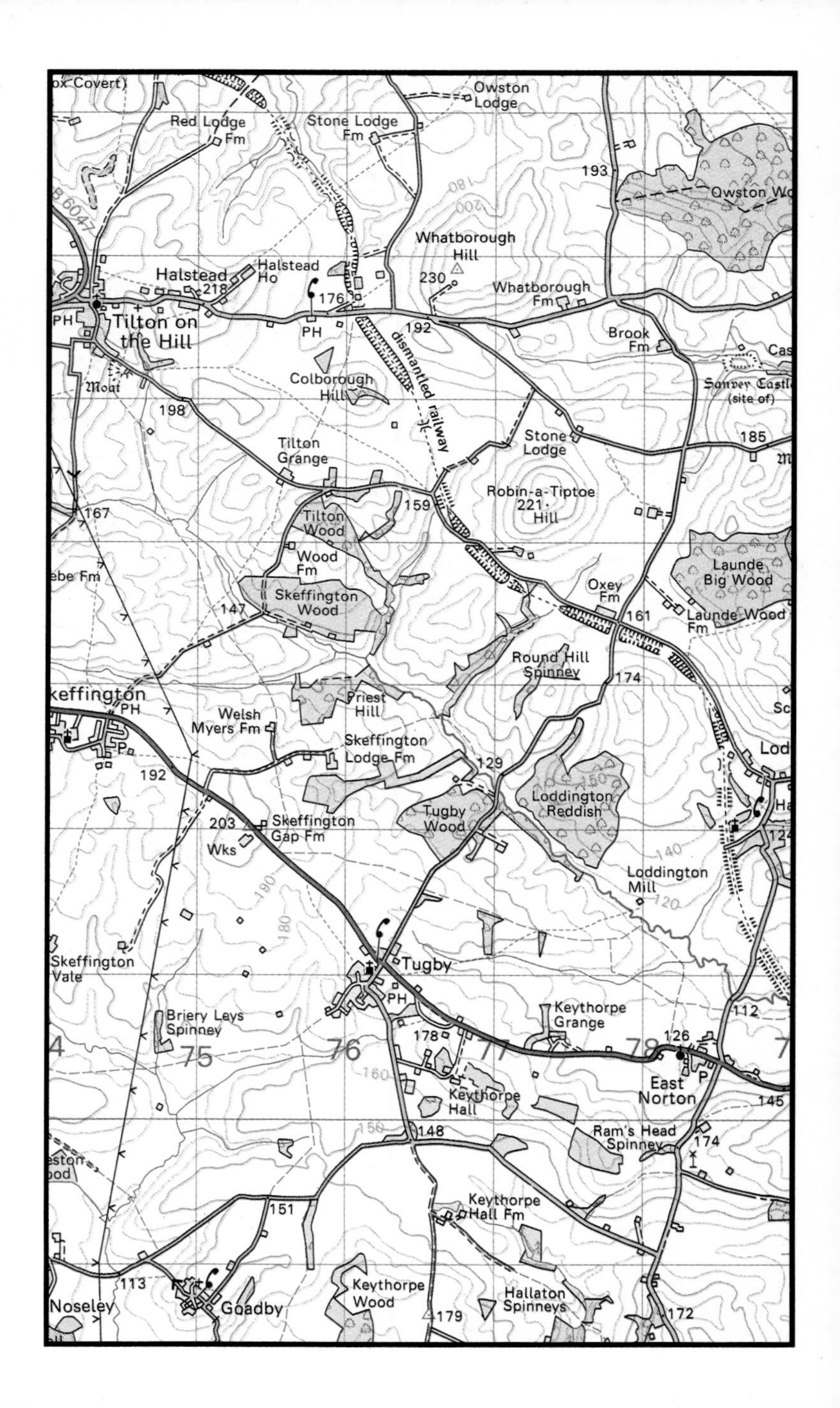

Owston Lodge
Red Lodge Fm
Stone Lodge Fm
193
Owston Wo
B 6047
Whatborough Hill
230
Halstead
Halstead Ho
218
176
Whatborough Fm
PH
Tilton on the Hill
PH
192
Brook Fm
dismantled railway
Colborough Hill
Moat
Sauvey Castle (site of)
198
Stone Lodge
185
Tilton Grange
Robin-a-Tiptoe Hill
221
159
167
Tilton Wood
Wood Fm
Launde Big Wood
Skeffington Wood
147
Oxey Fm
161
Launde Wood Fm
Round Hill Spinney
174
Skeffington
PH
Priest Hill
Welsh Myers Fm
Skeffington Lodge Fm
129
192
Loddington Reddish
Tugby Wood
203
Skeffington Gap Fm
Wks
Loddington Mill
120
140
150
190
180
Skeffington Vale
Tugby
PH
Keythorpe Grange
Briery Leys Spinney
178
112
126
75
76
77
78
160
Keythorpe Hall
East Norton
145
150
148
Ram's Head Spinney
174
151
Keythorpe Hall Fm
113
Keythorpe Wood
Hallaton Spinneys
Noseley
Goadby
179
172

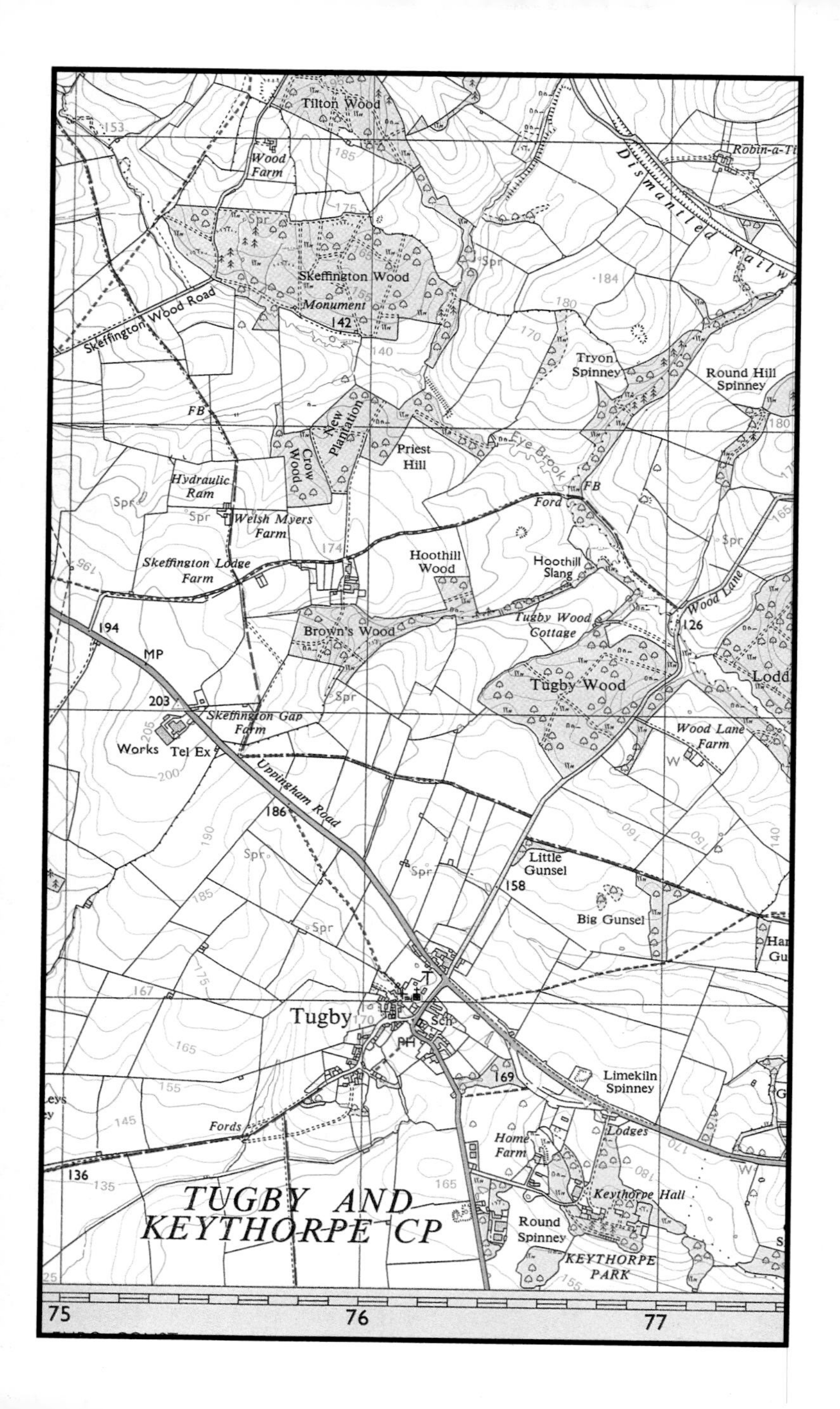

Tilton Wood
Wood Farm
Dismantled Railw
Robin-a-Ti
Skeffington Wood
Monument
Skeffington Wood Road
Tryon Spinney
Round Hill Spinney
New Plantation
Crow Wood
Priest Hill
Eye Brook
FB
Ford
Hydraulic Ram
Welsh Myers Farm
Skeffington Lodge Farm
Hoothill Wood
Hoothill Slang
Wood Lane
Tugby Wood Cottage
Brown's Wood
Tugby Wood
MP
Skeffington Gap Farm
Works
Tel Ex
Wood Lane Farm
Uppingham Road
Little Gunsel
Big Gunsel
Tugby
Sch
PH
Limekiln Spinney
Fords
Home Farm
Lodges
Keythorpe Hall
Round Spinney
KEYTHORPE PARK
TUGBY AND KEYTHORPE CP
75
76
77

Pathfinder
1:25 000

ROADS AND PATHS

M 1 or A 6(M) — Motorway

A 31(T) — Trunk or Main road

B 3074 — Secondary road

A 35 — Dual carriageway

Road generally more than 4m wide

Road generally less than 4m wide

Other road, drive or track

Unfenced roads and tracks are shown by pecked lines

Path

PUBLIC RIGHTS OF WAY

Public paths: Footpath; Bridleway

Byway open to all traffic

Road used as a public path

RAILWAYS

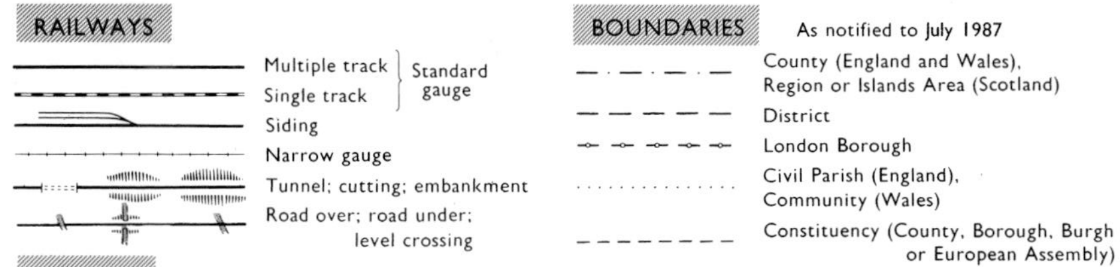

Multiple track; Single track (Standard gauge)

Siding

Narrow gauge

Tunnel; cutting; embankment

Road over; road under; level crossing

SYMBOLS

Place of worship: with tower; with spire, minaret or dome; without such additions

Building; important building

Glasshouse; youth hostel

Bus or coach station

Lighthouse; beacon

Triangulation pillar

T; A; R — Telephone: public; AA; RAC

Sloping masonry

pylon pole — Electricity transmission line

W Spr — Well, Spring

Site of antiquity

1066 — Site of battle (with date)

Gravel pit

Sand pit

Other pit or quarry

Refuse or slag heap

Loose rock

Boulders

Outcrop

Scree

Cliff

Water

Mud

Sand; sand & shingle

National Park or Forest Park Boundary

NT — National Trust always open

NT — National Trust opening restricted

NTS NTS — National Trust for Scotland

BOUNDARIES

As notified to July 1987

County (England and Wales), Region or Islands Area (Scotland)

District

London Borough

Civil Parish (England), Community (Wales)

Constituency (County, Borough, Burgh or European Assembly)

VEGETATION

Limits of vegetation are defined by positioning of the symbols but may be delineated also by pecks or dots

Coniferous trees

Non-coniferous trees

Coppice

Orchard

Scrub

Bracken, rough grassland

In some areas bracken ( ) and rough grassland ( ) are shown separately

Heath

Shown collectively as rough grassland on some sheets

Reeds

Marsh

Saltings

HEIGHTS

50 · ; 285 · — Determined by: ground survey; air survey

Surface heights are to the nearest metre above mean sea level. Heights shown close to a triangulation pillar refer to the station height at ground level and not necessarily to the summit

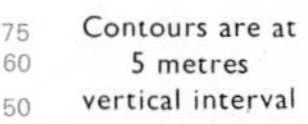

Contours are at 5 metres vertical interval

become popular because they are cheaper than leather but still have adequate ventilation.

Walking boots support the ankles but walking shoes are preferred by some people who don't like to have their ankles muffled—or don't like to look conspicuous on a gentle walk round the village! Walking shoes feel lighter than boots, and a good pair should have stout soles with a grip.

Checklist for buying boots:

- Buy from a specialist who will let you take time over fitting.
- Try on boots before midday because your feet may have swollen later on.
- Try on boots wearing a thick pair of socks—the shop assistant should offer you these.
- When laced, the boot should hold the back of your foot firmly so that it does not slide forward when going downhill. Your big toe should not be pressing against the boot's toe.
- The sole of the boot should be flexible and at least 12mm (½ inch) thick.
- A scree cuff will stop the boot rubbing your ankle and keep out small stones.
- A padded tongue will help to prevent the boot rubbing the top of your foot; a bellows tongue will help keep the water out.

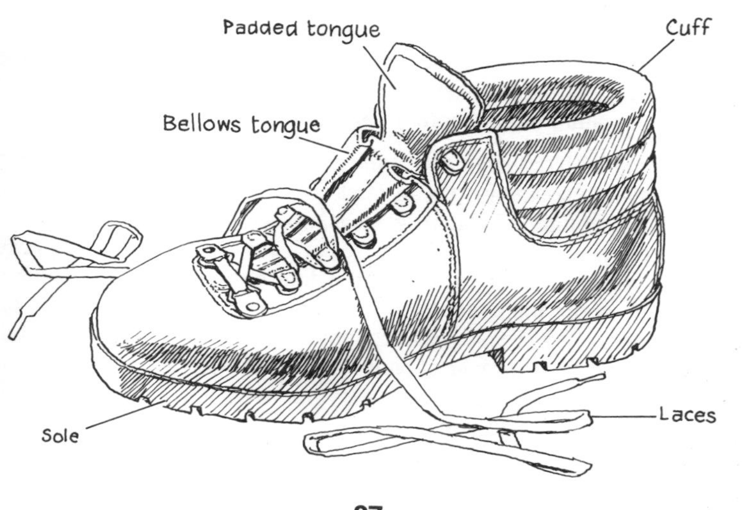

Leather boots and shoes are not waterproof. When you come back from a muddy walk, wash all the mud off and fill boots with crumpled paper to let them dry gradually, away from heat. When dry, the leather needs to be treated with a wax like Dubbin or Nikwax—or whatever the manufacturer recommends.

Wellingtons are waterproof and can be suitable for a short wet walk, but choose a pair that does not come too high up your leg. They can be very tiring to walk in. Although wellies are waterproof (until punctured) the rain can come down into them and there is nothing worse than a welly full of water.

Bog Trotter wellies have short legs, a good grip on the sole, and lacing round the top so that you can tighten them round your calves. This is quite useful as it helps to keep out mud and water—but it does not, of course, stop the rain running down your trousers and into your socks.

Trainers or running shoes are fine for a dry country walk on good tracks. They are also versatile, as you can use them for many other sports. They have good soles, but are not waterproof and do not support your ankles. Trainers can cost as much as boots, and you may not want to risk spoiling them on a muddy walk.

Whatever your choice of footwear, you will be lucky if you manage to avoid blisters altogether. Most walkers have suffered from them at one time or another, and everyone has their own personal remedy. Some people put plasters on the places where they know they are likely to get blisters before they set out, others carry plasters with them. It is best to use breathable waterproof plasters, rather than fabric ones, which tend to rub. The new Micropore surgical tape is also very effective. Try not to let the blister burst until you get home and can attend to it properly. And if you have forgotten to take plasters with you, don't take your boots off—it may be too painful to put them on again!

Experimenting with different socks might solve the problem of blisters. The best walking socks are those made of thick wool with no seams. (Beware cheap imitations constructed as a tube with a seam across the most sensitive part of your toe joints!) Specialist walking socks are very expensive, made with looped wool and nylon to provide a good padding for your feet. Some manufacturers recommend that no inner socks be worn with them. (Whereas I was brought up to use an inner pair of thin cotton socks and an outer pair of hand-made thick woollen ones.) Again, everyone has their own preference—try out various combinations until you have found what suits you best.

Waterproofs

A waterproof jacket is essential equipment. (Check that it is not merely showerproof—and make sure there is a hood with drawcords.) It should have zipped or press studded pockets for money and keys, and an inner pocket is useful for keeping papers dry. I like unzipped pockets for my hands when cold.

To begin with you may not want to spend too much—or you could manage with a jacket that you have already got. But once you start to take walking seriously you may wish to consider one of the very good, expensive anoraks which 'breathe'. In cheaper versions you can end up as wet inside from condensation as you would have done from the rain outside. When buying look for breathable cloth, and consider the weight and the foldability. I always look for one that isn't too noisy or stiff.

A jacket or anorak should ideally be long enough to cover your bottom. A two-way zip which allows you to open up the bottom of the jacket is useful when you are climbing high stiles, or when you are trying to reach your trouser pockets.

For winter walking a really good waterproof is worth its weight in gold. (You can proof material yourself with various commercial products and with varying degrees of success.)

In summer an anorak is going to spend most of its time in your rucksack, but even if it doesn't rain, a lightweight anorak or cagoule has many uses—for sitting on grass which is almost always damp even in fine weather, for wrapping round sandwiches to keep them cool, for enveloping your camera in case you fall in the canal, as well as for protection from the odd shower or chill wind.

Overtrousers

Most walkers hate them but carry them in their rucksacks to be worn for the minimum amount of time on the few occasions when they really work. They are a nuisance to put on (zips at the foot of the legs are essential if you don't want to have to remove your boots) and most are too heavy and constricting. However, when walking in the winter it can be a good idea to protect your trousers with an extra layer, so they are worth considering.

In warm weather you don't need to worry too much about getting damp, but there is nothing to beat overtrousers to take you through a field of

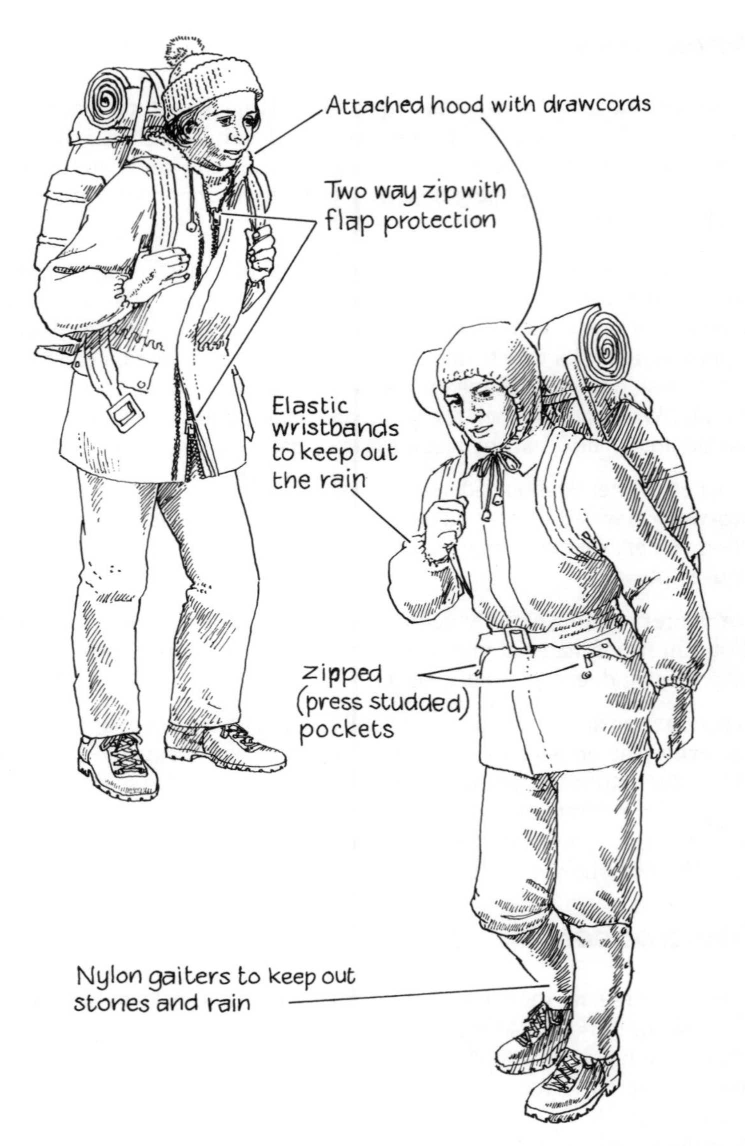

dew-drenched high crops in summer. (I have tried walking behind an open umbrella held low. It does not work! If you decide overtrousers are not worth the bother, you could try draping a cagoule like an apron round your knees to protect you through a field or two. This is quite effective.)

Bare legs dry quicker than trousers, but they do not stop the rainwater dripping down your socks, and you get stung by nettles!

Gaiters are useful for keeping the water off your socks. But check:

- Are they lightweight, and easy to store?
- How quickly can you get them on and off?
- How comfortable do you feel in them?
- Do they come too high up your legs?
- Are they going to prove worth the expense?

I have seen gaiters made from the cut-off ends of old mackintosh sleeves, threaded with elastic at top and bottom to make neat little cuffs to protect the ankles of socks. The only problem was that they could not be pulled on or off over boots. The owners had to wear them all day, or stop for the laborious process of removing boots (not easy, even in dry weather!).

Warm clothing

Several layers of thin woollen clothing are more useful than one big thick jumper because they trap more air to insulate you and because you can add or subtract items as the temperature rises or falls. You can remove garments as you go faster and become hotter, or you can put on more when you sit in a cool breeze or walk through woodland or shady or windy places.

Glossy walking magazines advertise a whole variety of clothing, but with common sense and a general awareness of the problems you are likely to encounter when walking, you can make do with your normal clothing, as long as you have good comfortable footwear and waterproof outerwear.

My own policy is to demote cotton and wool shirts, jumpers and trousers through a hierarchy of: for best, for going to work, for housework, gardening, painting and decorating—until they reach the walking stage. (But that is because I know I'm going to be scrambling through obstacles and investigating little-used paths. When walking less hazardous routes or visiting smarter places your hierarchy may well be different.)

Headgear

You lose most heat through your head, so it is only sensible in winter to make sure your head and ears are kept warm and cosy. Most anoraks have hoods, but an inner woolly hat is extra comforting.

In very hot weather you need to protect your head and neck from the sun. A light headscarf or a cotton sunhat does not take up much room and may save you from sunstroke, or from making you wish you had stayed at home on a hot day.

Clothing is a personal choice. Dress to suit yourself, and your walking style. Many of my friends always look smart for walking, even at the end of a muddy scramble. One of the smartest is kitted out completely from an Age Concern shop (total cost £4): another spends a small fortune on purchasing the top brand names from the adverts in the outdoor pursuits magazines.

You will soon realise that you don't have to compete in sartorial elegance when walking in the country. The really smart thing is to be dry, warm or cool and comfortable. But above all, wear clothes that you like wearing—woolly hats and orange cagoules are not compulsory!

2.2 Equipment

Rucksacks

You do not need to spend a lot of money on a rucksack. If it is comfortable and the right size, it doesn't need to be waterproof, provided you wrap everything inside in plastic bags. (You could even try the alternative method of encasing the whole rucksack in a plastic dustbin liner with holes cut for rucksack arm straps, as an American friend does. He learnt the trick from a famous energy conservationist, Amory Lovins, who spent a summer vacation as a Hiking Counsellor at a summer camp for young Americans in the 1970s. 'Uncle Amory' taught the kids many useful tricks of the walking trade and cutting armholes in black plastic bags to cover rucksacks was one of them. You might get a few odd looks though!)

If the rucksacks are all folded and packed tightly in the shop, ask to have one opened so that you can see how much it holds. Stuff it full of whatever you have handy (handbag, jacket or shoes) or take a selection of kit with you to put in it. Then try it on to see if it is comfortable.

Or if that seems a lot of trouble, ask friends for their recommendations. They may let you try on their rucksacks and give you helpful advice.

Checklist for buying a rucksack:

- Decide what size you need—rucksacks are measured in litres, and you shouldn't need more than 40l for a day walk.
- How many outside pockets do you need?
- Does it need to be showerproof?
- Do you want a frame? (See below for tips on packing a rucksack without a frame.)
- Will nylon or cotton material be sufficient or do you want a stronger rucksack in a heavier material?

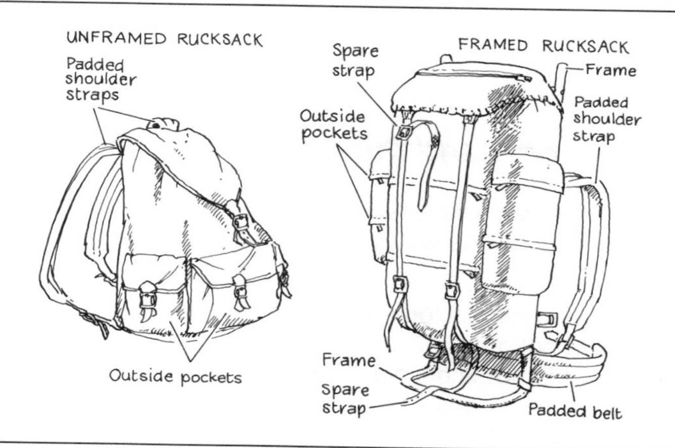

Tips for packing a rucksack:

- Spread the weight evenly so that the rucksack is not unbalanced.
- If you have a rucksack without a frame, make sure that you put something soft where the rucksack will rest on your back.
- Take care not to put anything valuable in outside pockets—to avoid having it stolen.
- Put the items you are likely to need first or most frequently at the top of the rucksack.
- If your rucksack is not showerproof, wrap vulnerable items in polythene bags.

Umbrellas

Do not despise the umbrella! It is no use in windy weather and a thorough nuisance when climbing stiles, but it is a great comfort in a really heavy downpour on a clear track and can be a boon when map reading in the rain.

Walking sticks

Devotees of walking sticks stride along roads and tracks with a very jaunty air. They claim that a stick helps them over really rough terrain, is useful for sounding out the solid ground under mud, nettles and ditches, or for waving at animals. As Lucretia Clark said: a strong stick is better than an umbrella.

Useful items and things you don't need

If you were walking on a desert island and could only take eight useful items and one luxury, which of the following would you choose?

- food (emergency food bars, fruit, chocolate, nuts)
- flask of hot drink
- screw-top bottle of cold drink
- plastic lunch bags
- map and map case
- compass
- useful bag for money, keys, comb, perfume
- paper tissues
- pencil and paper
- medical kit (blister pack, plasters, insect repellent, vaseline, suncream, antiseptic cream)
- nail file
- string
- safety pins
- spare boot laces
- tape recorder
- camera
- binoculars
- radio

If you ask friends to turn out their rucksacks you will discover an amazing variety of items they consider important enough to carry around, despite the weight and inconvenience. I have one friend who travels the world with what she wears and what she carries in her hand luggage, which seems to consist of a toothbrush and money. Whereas another boasts that she can provide from her pack any item that anyone has ever needed. Her pack does not look any heavier than mine.

An exercise in positive choice of what to carry is a useful discipline for the walker. It is essential for backpacking holidays and also useful for day walks where you may find no shops. If you are going to carry your own belongings you will want to think about ways of lessening their weight. Family-size packets are out. Boxes and containers are out. You can extract just the amount you need and put it in a small tube or in a plastic bag. You can cut off the ends of toothbrushes to save weight and space, and take the last remaining fraction of a tube of toothpaste or bar of soap. You may decide to take a lightweight thermos flask and leave out the radio and the library book. On the other hand if you plan a couple of hours by a river halfway through your walk, a book might be worth its weight.

You need to decide the minimum amount and maximum weight you wish to carry to keep life comfortable and pleasant in relation to where you are going and what sort of walking you are going to do. Make your own list of essentials, then cut it down to the bare minimum. Be ruthless, but not reckless!

A good tip is one I learnt from a friend taking a school party youth hostelling: 'Know the geography of your rucksack. Remember where you keep each item. Don't sit on the banana.'

2.3 Companions

> Nature's particular gift to the walker—a gift no other form of exercise seems to transmit in the same degree—it is to set the mind jogging, to make it garrulous, exalted, a little mad, maybe . . . Then everything seems to join in, sun, wind, the white road and the dusty hedges, the spirit of the season, whichever that may be, the friendly old earth that is pushing forth life of every sort under your feet . . . till you walk in the midst of a blessed company, immersed in dream talk far transcending any possible human conversation.
>
> Kenneth Grahame, *Dream Days*

Walking alone does not necessarily feel lonely. It is on the occasions when I walk alone that I meet the fox that walks with me, unafraid, or the owl in the hedgerow, blinking at me in the daylight. Alone, you see more, notice more; you collect your own thoughts; calm your disquiets; relax your tensions. I would never be deterred from walking for lack of a friend at my side. I would just make sure I kept my wits about me and took sensible precautions.

On one wintry solo walk, I remember lying for some time in agony on icy ground until I recovered from an unwise jump across a frozen stream (after being forced into a detour because of a missing bridge). I made several vows then, about not taking risks—such as jumping across streams—when walking alone. Like Dorothy Wordsworth, I swore: 'I shall never go alone in rough places and on unknown ground late in the evening' (Letters of William and Dorothy Wordsworth, October 1810.) . . . or in the depths of winter.

If you are worried about your safety you could leave details of your route with a friend, relative or neighbour and give an estimated time of return. This would speed up a police search if anything did happen to you. But if you feel it is excessively fussy to worry someone else about a very unlikely accident you could compromise by leaving the information on the kitchen table or in the diary by the phone.

Many people believe that you should never walk alone. The accepted rule for mountain and moorland walking is that you need a group of five for safety: two to stay with an injured person and two to run for help. But this is not so for country walking, where the perils are few and far between.

If you do not like the idea of solitary walking, look for a good companion. A friend can double the pleasure: and choosing a congenial companion for walking is not as difficult as for many other activities.

- You do not need to talk much, so it doesn't matter if you disagree about politics, child-rearing or religion.
- You don't have to like the same food. You can have independent picnics.
- You can usually reach a compromise about speed and distance.
- You do not have to share the same interests, provided you each have a tolerant attitude towards whatever the other finds fascinating and

are willing to wait while they take photographs, or examine rare species, or pursue their favourite line of enquiry.

- You can each have a separate map and guide book and still be companionable, provided you agree on a route or agree to separate and meet again at intervals. (In fact it is much more satisfactory if you do each have your own. Two heads are better than one when it comes to navigating and a map is very difficult to share.)

If you have no conveniently available friend or if you do not want the bother of planning a walk and navigating yourself, you might prefer to walk as a member of a group, so that someone else can choose the itinerary and take the responsibility for your well-being!

Groups

There are walking groups in most towns or villages, ranging from nationally-known associations like the Ramblers, Holiday Fellowship, or the Youth Hostel Association to smaller local rambling groups or footpath preservation societies. There are also many informal walking groups, some of them specially arranged for young girls and boys, or for families, retired people, or the unemployed.

Educational courses on wildlife, archeology and geology (such as those run by the WEA for adults) often include short walks and introduce you to other people with a shared interest in the country and in walking. You could find out details of classes and groups from your library or information centre and make your choice from what is available in your locality.

If you choose to walk with a rambling group you will be expected to follow certain informal rules such as keeping behind the leader and not rushing ahead; not wandering off on your own; checking that the last one shuts the gate; and letting someone know if you decide to loiter for any reason, so that they will wait for you. There might be a strict rule that all dogs should be kept on leads.

If you are the leader of a group, even if it is only your own family, you will probably feel obliged to take more care with your planning, your escape routes, stopping places and estimates of distance and timing, as well as the emergency supplies you carry, because you will feel responsible for their comfort and enjoyment. For your peace of mind, it might be a good idea to let the others know what you expect of them and what they can, and cannot, expect of you.

Guidelines for leaders

(A discussion document—you might like to modify it for your group.)

- Pre-walk the route if you can, to check that it is passable and suitable.
- Tell the group what to expect in the way of terrain and stopping places.
- Inform them of any possible escape routes, if you feel they need that reassurance.
- Check at the beginning of the walk that everyone is properly kitted out.
- Count the number of your group. If it is large, you may feel it is necessary to appoint a 'back stop' or 'tail-end Charlie' to shepherd the group along and shut gates.
- Give instructions about shutting all gates. (Or open and shut them yourself. This provides quite a good opportunity to count your group and check that they are all surviving: but make sure they wait for you to lead them on again!)
- Pace your walking so that you can keep the group together. Tell them not to race ahead or to straggle behind, but to keep in sight and calling distance of you or the person in front of them. Encourage them to take responsibility for one another.
- Count the group at intervals and at the end of the walk. (These numbers should tally with the number you had at the beginning! If you have more it matters less than if you have fewer!) It is very embarrassing for a leader to lose anyone—and it's not much fun for the one who is lost!

3 ON YOUR WAY

3.1 Signs and waymarks

You may be lucky enough to find a beautifully signposted and immaculately maintained route all the way to your next destination. If you are walking a well-trodden path you may not even need your map to guide you.

You will need it, however, if you wish to be intelligent about the area you are walking through, to know the names of places around you and to be aware of things in the landscape that you might not otherwise notice (like the site of an ancient settlement, a Roman villa, a deserted medieval village, a burial ground, a treasure hoard, the scene of a battle, or the remains of an old hovel or pond).

And you will need it if you are leaving the waymarked route at any point. Many new paths are now waymarked. A parish decides to create a jubilee path; a philanthropic landowner decides to dedicate a permissive path; a railway society buys land and converts a length of old track into a public right of way; a historical action group succeeds in opening a path which has lain unrecorded for centuries; a heritage preservation society reinstates an approach to an ancient monument; nature conservationists donate a stretch of woodland . . . and all these paths are provided with fine new waymark signs.

It is easy to become hypnotised by these signs and to follow them to a place not on your itinerary. You need to be aware, too, that waymark signs can disappear, be vandalised or accidently damaged. It is wise not to rely on them alone, even on a national long distance path. Check with your map.

3.2 Map and compass

> I am told there are people who do not care for maps, and find it hard to believe. The names, the shapes of the woodlands, the courses of the roads and rivers, the prehistoric footsteps of man still distinctly traceable up hill and down dale, the mills and the ruins, the ponds and the ferries, perhaps the Standing Stone or the Druidic Circle on the heath; here is an inexhaustible fund of interest for any one with eyes to see and twopence worth of imagination to understand with.
>
> R L Stevenson *Essays*

Before you set off, it helps to make sure you have your map folded so that your route is visible. You may need to stop later to refold it so that you can see the next section, but at least you can start off prepared for action. Keep the map in a plastic bag or mapcase to protect it from thumbprints, mud, sweat, rain and river water!

If you want to use a compass, you can set it the night before, too. The Silva type is the easiest to use with a map.

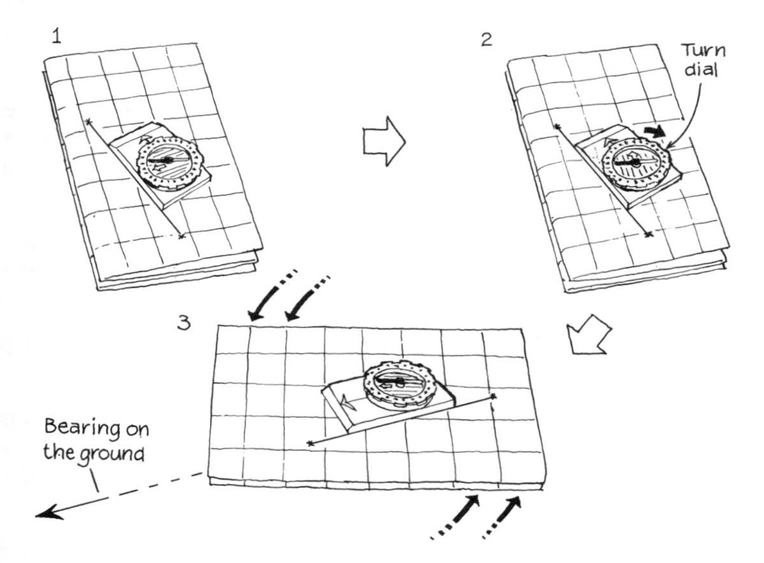

Place the edge of the baseplate on your map so that it connects the point you are starting from and the point you are aiming for. Turn the dial so that the orienting lines on the transparent bottom are parallel with grid lines running N–S on the map, the direction arrow pointing north. Then turn the whole compass, plus map, until the red end of the magnetic needle points to north.

When you set off on your walk, all you have to do is hold your compass with the red needle over the arrow which points to north. The direction arrow for you to follow is then pointing to the way you want to go.

You will need to reset the compass whenever the path changes direction (and watch out—you might not notice this if it is gradual!). But at least if you are ready for the start of the walk you can save time and trouble at this crucial stage in map reading, which may boost your confidence for the rest of your walk.

Map references

You might occasionally find it useful to give someone an exact map reference, if for instance you are arranging a meeting place, perhaps for dry socks, hot food or transport home.

Decide on the place where you want to meet. If possible, make it somewhere distinctive, like a pub, church, telephone box or road junction, and write down the numbers of the map lines which intersect near to it. The numbers are written at the top or bottom of the page and in the side margins.

Start at the bottom of your map. Go from the side margin and move towards the centre of the map until you reach a vertical line at the west side of your destination. Find the number of this line (in the margin at the top or bottom of the map). Write down the number (or memorise it).

Then go up the map until you meet the line below your chosen point. Write down the number of this horizontal line (from the side margin of the map).

You can give a rough guide with these four numbers. The pub on the map is in square 73 11.

To be more accurate it is usual to give a six figure reference. To do this divide the edges of the square into 10, and count how far into the square your landmark is. The pub is about 3⁄10 along and 5⁄10 up the square. Thus the pub on the map is at 733115.

The way to remember this method of giving a map reference is: 'Go INTO the house before you go UPstairs.' That is, go INTO the map (and give that number) before you go UP it (to the next number).

Give this map reference number to the person meeting you and check that they have a map and have found the right place. (If necessary, tell them to go INTO the map first and then UP. Many people give map references the wrong way. It is no good you getting it right, if they don't! Ask them to write the reference number down and mark the place on their map. Time and care taken at this stage might save a lot of time and aggravation later.)

You can use this system of giving a map reference for reporting obstructions and difficulties to your footpath officers, which can save you a lengthy description. If, for instance, there are obstructions at the hedge in the first field, the stream and the fort, you need only give the map references for them to be able to find the place you mean.

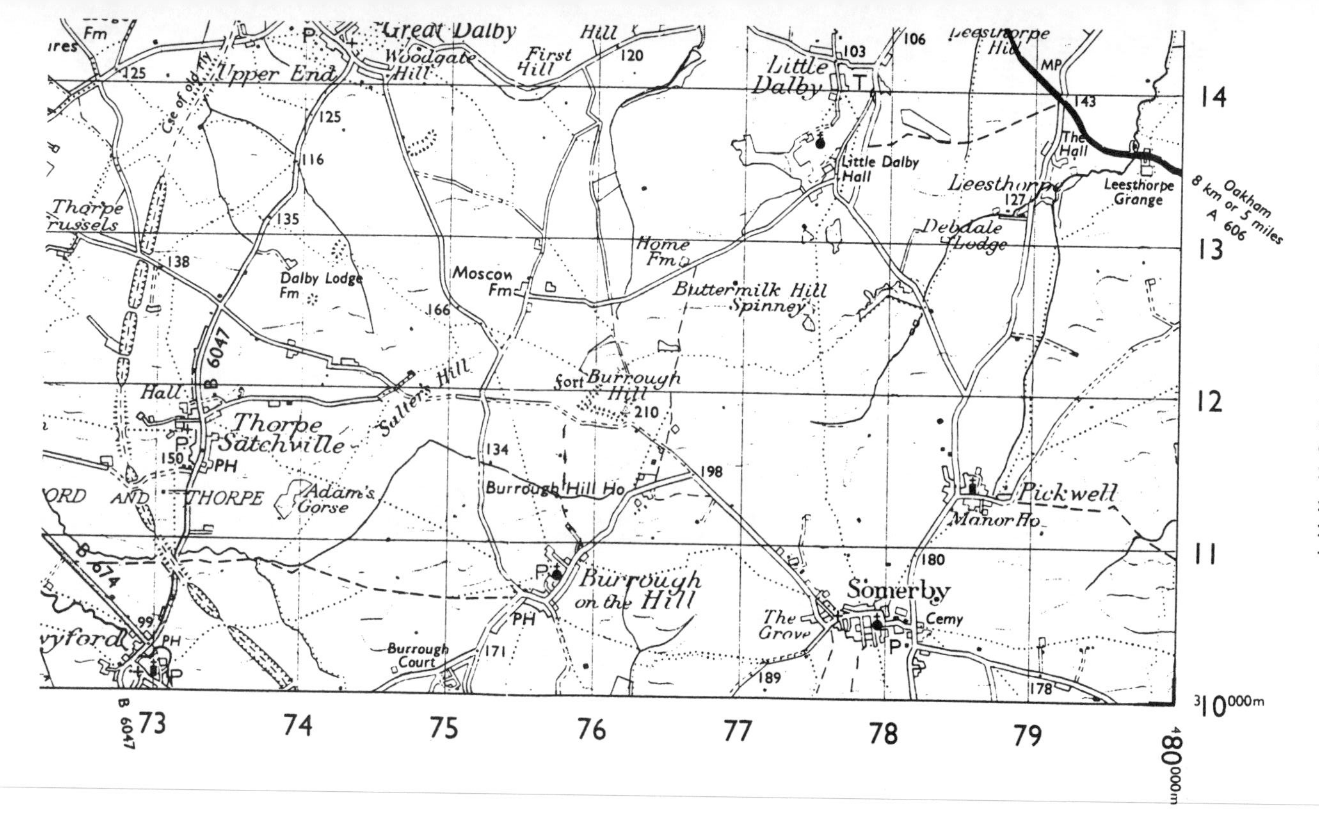
Great Dalby
Woodgate Hill
First Hill
Upper End
Cse of old Rly
Little Dalby
Little Dalby Hall
Leesthorpe Hill
MP
The Hall
Leesthorpe
Leesthorpe Grange
Oakham 8 km or 5 miles A 606
Debdale Lodge
Thorpe Trussels
Dalby Lodge Fm
Moscow Fm
Home Fm
Buttermilk Hill Spinney
Fort Burrough Hill
Salter's Hill
Hall
Thorpe Satchville
PH
B 6047
Adam's Gorse
THORPE
Burrough Hill Ho
Pickwell
Manor Ho
Burrough on the Hill
Somerby
Cemy
The Grove
Burrough Court
B 674
14
13
12
11
73
74
75
76
77
78
79
310000m
480000m

Using your map

Most people find it easier to hold their map in the way they are walking, so that they are heading UP the map. (Many simplified maps do this for you, drawing the map upside down when they know you want to walk south!)

It helps if you can keep your thumb on the place you have reached and keep moving it along as you walk. If your thumb isn't long enough to reach the far side of your map, you can improvise with a marker (I use a magnifying glass case or a compass).

Some people actually draw on their map or their map case with a highlighter pen, which does save time in locating your route as you walk along. (But it messes up your map or map case.)

Anything to speed up the map reading process is a help because it gives you more time to concentrate on the countryside around you and the people who are with you.

3.3 Reading the landscape

Once you have planned your route and reached your starting place, and parked your vehicle somewhere sensible (a village car park, if possible, a pub car park if the publican is willing, or a wide bit of road where you do not block a gateway or cause a hazard to others), look carefully for the start of your path.

An ideal path might start from near the church or pub, then go in a direct line to the next village, past an old mill perhaps, and across a stream before going up a hill which gives a fine view over the next valley, enabling you to aim straight for the next church spire. But not all are as straightforward as this!

The start of a path needs special care. If you are lucky the path will be signposted from the road, but you still need to check carefully that it is the path you want and that it is going to your next destination. If you have a compass you can orientate yourself in relation to north and check that the church is on the correct side of your path and that you are walking in the right direction.

If the path is not signposted you can start looking for likely openings near the church or between houses on the village street or in the new housing development. There may be a post with a No Cycling symbol, which means it is a footpath. There may be a dead end road or a wide track with a gate leading into open fields. In wild hill and moorland country you have only your compass for a guide but for country walking you usually have the added benefit of hedges and walls to keep you in the right direction.

When you are launched into the open fields, with hedges and walls for guides, you can orientate yourself with your compass and check that you are where you hope you are, by looking carefully at the position and shape of the fields. You then need to keep your eyes open for the crossing places in hedges or walls ahead of you, checking all the time that field boundaries are in the right place, according to your map.

Following a well trodden path

You learn to note signs of previous walkers: their bootmarks; their sweet wrappers and empty crisp packets (tut tut!); the single file lines they have made through crops; the slithering marks in the grass at the other side of the ditch they have jumped; the places they have gone through hedges and where they have cut the barbed wire or constructed a crossing over the stream.

With experience you learn to sense where generations of feet are likely to have walked: along contours, valleys, hill ridges; towards church spires and landmark hills or to visible features on the skyline, and through gaps in barrier walls. You learn to note the tall trees standing out like sentinels, marking the place where the stile or fence is hidden in the hedge.

You begin to notice old gateposts and gates leaning unused in the hedgerows where they fell, and old plank crossings and large stones used for many years as footstools for stiles over fences. You note the places where generations of barbed wire have been cut by walkers and patched by farmers so that you see the rusty old pieces joined by new with a linking knot. These confirm that you are on a used path.

Ancient routes

Most paths are old: some are older than others. (See section 4.2 on History of paths.)

If your path goes in a direct line to a distant landmark, perhaps a hill with a name indicating that it was once a ritual meeting place for worship, burial, trade, defence, habitation or justice; or if it goes beside a continuous hedge joining two villages or towns in a straight line, you can be pretty sure it is an ancient track. If you find old slate or stone footbridges or bits of old paved route, you can also deduce that you are on an old route.

If you come to a sharp bend in the road, where the footpath goes straight on you can tell you are at the site of a road route change, where the footpath might well be the older of the two routes. On old maps, present day footpaths and bridleways are often shown as roads. Modern roads sometimes follow the old ways but sometimes bypass them, leaving the old roads as minor lanes or footpaths.

Many old footpaths took right-angled bends where they went beside the edges of medieval cultivated fields. You may be able to note the pattern of ridge and furrow where the ploughing has marked the landscape. You may find the path follows the junction of ridges that go in different directions and that you are walking along the old turning headland for the ox-drawn ploughs.

On the other hand, you may come to places where the lie of the land has been so disturbed that you cannot see where the older lines of the footpaths lay.

3.4 Problems

You may choose to walk in areas of the country where paths are not well-maintained and not well-walked. If you do so you might meet problems that used to be common before access to the countryside became acknowledged as a high priority issue.

Before waymarking came into fashion (in the 1970s) and before the 1990 Rights of Way Act, serious walkers expected to find their way blocked in all sorts of ways. It was part of the exercise: it came with the joy. You couldn't expect pleasure without suffering. We were a puritanical lot!

But now, as walkers, we expect paths to be well-maintained and we are perhaps less well-prepared for problems and difficulties. I therefore feel obliged to point out some which may occur and hope that they will not spoil your walk if they do!

Changes on the map

Your map may be out of date. New roads may have been built. Modern roads are sometimes constructed over old green ways, and you may be obliged to walk along roads that are marked as mere paths on your map.

Motorways have a nasty habit of cutting a completely new swathe of country to avoid towns, villages and congested traffic routes. A new motorway drives its way ruthlessly through the countryside, going directly across footways and bridleways and ancient green lanes.

You may find your path diverted alongside a noisy motorway which spoils your views and fills your lungs with lead poisoning. After crossing an impressive bridge you may have to make your way back beside the same unattractive highway to regain the point where the path was diverted.

A new road changes the whole look of a landscape and can disorientate the walker. When a motorway or huge bypass appears, it is difficult to keep your place on the map, either because so many hedges and walls have been removed or because two paths may have been combined, in the interests of efficiency, and you are obliged to take an alternative route.

Railways and canals

In the last century, railways and canals often disturbed the original line of a path in the way that motorways do now.

Sometimes footbridges and level crossings were provided for the footpath, but occasionally paths were legally diverted to the nearest alternative crossing. Sometimes, however, no provision was written in to the sale of land to the railway or canal company, and so you may occasionally find a path that comes to a dead end at a railway line or canal.

You may find it impossible to see where the route originally went. Even if you are able to discover it from old maps, you will find it difficult to claim that there is still a right of way across the line, despite the fact that there are paths on either side of it, leading to a non-existent crossing point. The documents of British Rail and the water companies are not easy to investigate when it comes to footpath matters. This makes it difficult when attempting to negotiate for the restoration of footpath rights.

Untrodden paths

One of the great problems in recent years has been the removal of hedges, subsidised by government in the name of efficient farming using bigger machines. A missing hedge is very confusing when you are relying on field boundaries for guidance. You do not always realise at first that it has been removed. When the field shape does not agree with your map, you need to look for the tell-tale signs of hedge removal. You can sometimes detect where the hedge boundary has changed. Is there an odd unexplained bend in the hedge, where another once joined it? Is there a slight ridge in the field where the hedge used to be? Is there one isolated tree or a line of old tree stumps standing in the middle of the field? These may be signs of old hedge lines. You need to use these clues because maps cannot keep up with the speed of change in farming practice at the moment.

Prairie fields and crops

A huge prairie field where several hedges have been removed and the whole area used for crops is a real challenge for a walker. You can still cross the field because the right of way remains but groups should walk in single file to minimise damage to the crops. Early in the growing season you can navigate your way across the field, keeping in the right direction and fixing your sights on a likely landmark. You are unlikely to be able to detect where the old hedges were because they have been so deeply ploughed out. When the crops are high you might have to admit defeat in the face of something impenetrable like broad beans or oilseed rape in full bloom. Many walkers give up at this point.

But do not despair! There are alternatives to battling your way through. See if there is any landmark on the far side of the field and work out a strategy for making your way round to it without exhausting yourself. At this point you may legitimately trespass. If there is an alternative, try it.

It is now an offence for a farmer to plough up a field path and not reinstate it. So, if you have any energy left when you reach home, you can vent some of your frustration in writing a letter of complaint to your footpath officer (see page 64).

Missing footbridges

A missing footbridge is sometimes even more of a problem. It is the responsibility of the local authority to see that bridges are kept in good order, but of course they are vulnerable constructions: floods wash them away; farmers damage them when deepening ditches with heavy new machinery; frosts break concrete plank bridges; old wooden bridges need constant repair.

Without a bridge a walker might have to choose between a risky jump or a long detour. A difficult choice! The risky jump is not to be recommended if you are walking alone. If you do break a limb or pull a muscle, you really need a friend. One friend alone may not be adequate transport home, but could at least go for help.

But making a detour can have its own problems, too. Before you set off on any diversion or detour from the path, it is wise to look carefully for an alternative safe crossing as near as possible to your original route. Try to work out how you can best regain the proper path because you need to return to it as soon as you can.

Dorothy Wordsworth's journal describes how after seeing William safely on his way one evening she lost her route back in the dark. She ended up in a trackless peat moss, going through a wood and over high dry stone walls and through a bog, stumbling on, often above the knees in mud, until she reached the safety of a cottage, where the wife lent her dry stockings.

Of course things aren't always as bad as this, but once off a path you cannot rely on finding unobstructed field exits or crossing places over streams. You may come to buildings or enclosures that bar your way completely and force you to turn back or go even further out of your way.

Bear in mind, too, that the wisest course sometimes may be to admit defeat and go back to your starting point! (You can always complain via your footpath officer once you get home!)

There has been great improvement in footpath maintenance in the last few years. Where these problems were once the rule, they are now the exception in many parts of the country. And long may this remain so!

4

RIGHTS OF WAY

> Many of us have a deep love of the countryside: we feel instinctively that its tranquillity and sense of history are part of our heritage. For most people therefore the rights of way network is a passport, a way in to a sanctuary to escape the pressures of everyday living.
>
> Sir Derek Barber, Chairman of the Countryside Commission to 1991

'But are there any paths nowadays? Aren't they all ploughed up?'
'The paths I walked when I was a child aren't there any more.'
'You have to walk on roads now and country roads are so dangerous. . . .'
'Why walk when you can go by car?'

These are the sort of remarks I hear when the subject of footpaths is raised. Many people say that they are saddened because their children and grandchildren are missing the simple pleasures and healthy exercise that they themselves had from walking in the country when they were young. They fear that paths have now been closed or have disappeared through neglect.

For town dwellers, the open fields are further away from the town centres than they used to be. Footpaths are now unfamiliar territory to people who are more used to roads and motorway signs than to stiles and hedges.

For country dwellers the familiar landscape has been changed beyond recognition by modern farming methods and new building, new roads, new landowners. The fields no longer seem welcoming to them. For newcomers to country walking it is often difficult to know where to start.

4.1 Where can I walk?

There is a vast network of footpaths, bridleways, byways and county roads or green lanes all over England and Wales, which are rights of way for all walkers. (Scotland has a slightly different system, with more open access. Any path that links two settlements and any path that has been in continuous use for 20 years is automatically deemed to be a public right of way.)

Your rights of way

Is it a private road, as it may say it is, or is it a public right of way? Is it a dead end farm track or an ancient route between villages? Does the PRIVATE NO TRESPASSERS sign mean we can't go along this drive?

Most of the time you will have no problems finding out the answers from your map. Rights of way are recorded on Ordnance Survey (OS) maps. If that 'PRIVATE ROAD' has a red dotted line or a green dotted line along it, then it is a right of way. If it only has black lines, it may not be, and you may need to use your creative map reading skills, or a trial and error method.

How to find out if a path is a right of way

Ancient common laws give you the right to walk any of these routes without hindrance. You can loiter long enough to take reasonable rest or refreshment, but must not trespass off the path.

Footpaths are for walkers. Theoretically you can take a pram or go in a wheelchair, but in practice you have to be prepared for obstacles like stiles, fences and kissing gates (which effectively bar the way for anything but the lightest of pushchairs) as these paths are not designed or intended for wheeled traffic.

Ideally, paths should be wide enough for two walkers to pass one another or for two walkers to walk companionably along, hand-in-hand into the sunset. In practice a single file track is the most you are likely to find in farming country.

Bridleways are for walkers, horse riders and cyclists. On a bridleway you should be able to pass through gates and not have to cross stiles. There should be enough room for two horse riders to pass and so walkers should not need to walk single file on these tracks, except to avoid horses or bikes!

Byways, county roads, green lanes and other 'roads used as public paths' are for walkers, horse riders and cyclists and for any vehicle that is prepared to risk its tyres and suspension on an unsurfaced way.

Creative map reading means looking at maps, old and new, and hypothesising where paths would have been likely to go when they were the main links between places. The alternative method of trial and error research requires time and energy of a different sort, an observation of signs which might indicate an ancient route or an obvious short cut. You need to be willing to retrace your steps if you are challenged—or a degree of charm and courage to convince any challenger that you believed this was a right of way. I do not recommend too much use of this method. It can be quite exhausting!

You can buy OS Pathfinder and Landranger maps at good book shops and some newsagents. (Look in your telephone book under *Maps and Charts* for the names of stockists.) Your library may also have copies that you can borrow. Tourist offices often provide good walking guides, but it is worth checking that they are up to date.

If you have problems with any path marked on your map you can check the route by looking at the definitive maps held at County Hall. These are the maps from which the Ordnance Survey gets its information.

There are very few rights of way that are not marked on definitive maps and, surprisingly enough, those few unmarked ones may be the byways, county roads and green lanes, which sound so solid and permanent and visible. On the contrary, these routes are sometimes less visible on the ground than footpaths, and you may find that they are not hedged or signposted or marked on your OS map. They often make good, quiet paths because so many can only be discovered after some research. You would need to check with the definitive map, possibly asking your rights of way officer for assistance in finding the details of county roads.

For paths close to your home in country districts you could ask your local parish clerk for a look at the definitive map held by your parish council. (The library or post office will probably give you the address of the parish clerk.)

If you find someone has built a bungalow or huge silo across your path, you can check with the definitive map to see whether the owner has had the path legally diverted and, if so, where it now goes. Paths are sometimes diverted to go round buildings or for special agricultural uses (like a pick-your-own farm or a trout fishery).

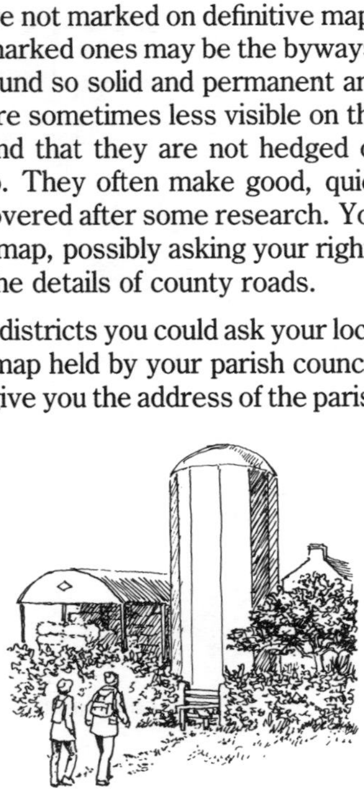

Any diversion should be clearly waymarked. Most diversion orders stipulate that a certain width be left for the path and you should look closely at your map to ensure that you are returned as soon as possible to the original route. (It is always confusing to follow a route which does not exactly agree with the map.)

If a path is legally diverted it is marked on the county council's definitive map, which is constantly updated, but it may be many years before it gets recorded onto new OS maps . . . and you may be using a very old OS map, so you should check with the definitive map before you accuse the farmer of obstruction.

If you do meet a misleading notice

or an obstructed path

write your letter of complaint to the rights of way officer in the local city or county hall rights of way department. It is their responsibility to see that paths are kept in good condition for public use.

Points to remember:

- A footpath or bridleway is as much part of the highway system as a main road is.
- The closure of a public path, like the closure of motorways, is a serious business.
- The obstruction of any highway is illegal. The planting of crops and the depositing of rubbish on the motorway or any other public right of way is not allowed.

4.2 History of paths

Most people hesitate to walk along a path across farmland. We think of the land as the farmer's garden or backyard, and to walk through their beautiful broad bean plants seems as rude as walking in our boots across their living-room carpet.

But we know that a footpath is a public right of way just as much as the motorway is, so perhaps we need to adjust our perspective and consider how we would feel about someone digging up a bit of the A1 or the M1 to plant geraniums. However much of an improvement this might be to our road system, no one would be allowed to block off the highway by cultivating it in this manner!

Our paths have been an important part of the highway system for hundreds, perhaps thousands, of years. History shows us that our paths were there before the land was ploughed. We know that people took these ancient routes to places of worship, and trade and war. We know that there were long distance routes along the high ridges before the Romans came. (Dig below a Roman road and you might find a Bronze Age track, as at Flag Fen, the Bronze Age village site excavated near Peterborough.)

We know about the impressive Roman roads such as Watling Street, Fosse Way and Gartree Road. They are often still clearly traceable as modern roads like the A5 and the A46. Where the modern roads bend away from the straight Roman route the old highway is often indicated by a dotted line on the map, though it may not be visible on the ground. Sometimes, however, it remains as a gated road, green lane, bridleway or footpath, so that we can still walk where the Romans marched.

We know that the Anglo-Saxons used these routes, because their settlements are often near the Roman roads and we know that they must have travelled regularly between the farms and villages that they gradually established. We have no maps to show these routes, but we have meticulous descriptions of land boundaries in old charters.

One land charter itemises land given by King Aethelbard for a monastery at Crediton in 739 AD. The boundary goes

> From the bridge to the highway, to the plough ford on the Exe, along the Exe to Luha's tree to the enclosure gate to Dodda's ridge to Grendel's pit, to ivy grove, to the ford at woodcock hollow, to fernbury, to eagle ridge. From eagle ridge to the ford in the wooded hollow, to Tettanburn, upstream to hilly brook . . . to the crab apple, to the green road to the wolf trap, upstream to where the watercourse divides, up the middle of the ridge and straight as a shaft to the alder, south over the precipice . . . to alder copse, to Brunwald's tree, to ash hollow . . . the deer pool . . . the rushy ford . . . wolf hollow . . . cress pool . . . pig hollow . . . hawk hollow . . . etc . . .
>
> The Anglo-Saxon Charter

In the days before maps, this is how routes would be described and handed down from generation to generation. It all sounds much more interesting than a list of map reference numbers such as we would now use!

From about 1770 we have maps that mark old roads that are often now barely visible as tracks over fields. Some of these must have been the main roads along which kings and queens made their progress through the land, holding court and demanding from lords and vassals rights of service and provisioning; and by bishops visiting their palaces. Later they may have been used by famous travellers such as Celia Fiennes, who rode on horseback on her travels in 1689; and Daniel Defoe, who made his *Tour Through the Whole Island of Great Britain* in 1724–6.

Many of these old roads can be detected only by those who have eyes trained to see the tell-tale signs of old highways. Old footpaths, of course, are even more likely to disappear than old roads.

Over the centuries we have lost many field paths because they were never mapped. We know that our own grandparents walked to village schools and neighbouring churches, mills and smithies, shops and pubs, on routes across fields that they had walked with their parents. Not all of these paths are marked now on definitive maps.

Some were not recorded when the land was enclosed—the Enclosure Acts tend to record only those paths which are to be used as access to individual plots of land. Before Enclosure the fields were large areas broken up into strips and separated from each other by a narrow piece of unploughed land, rather than by hedges or walls. Gradually the more powerful landowners acquired strips of land adjoining each other and planted hedges round them, or enclosed them. Enclosure continued right up to this century, when farmers and landowners began to realise the economic benefits of large open fields, with the result that the hedges were torn out again.

Some paths got mislaid when railways and canals were constructed. Some were missed off the map when parish councils were asked to register all their paths. County roads are often not recorded at all on OS maps because they do not come into the category of footpaths, bridleways or metalled roads, the only categories that OS acknowledges.

During the 20th century, many local footpath groups have been formed to save these and other rights of way for the public. Ordnance Survey began to record footpaths in 1900, though at first they added a disclaimer, stating that tracks and paths marked were not necessarily rights of way. Since the publication of the second series the situation has improved. Paths marked with a red or green line on OS Landranger and Pathfinder maps are now declared to be public rights of way.

There have been many deliberate attempts to close rights of way. In the past landowners have often denied access over their land unless it brought profit to their estate. You can find on the map many places where the network of paths has noticeable gaps. Paths that once linked villages were absorbed into the estates of landowners. And the green lines of public rights of way now stop abruptly at the edge of what has become private territory.

In open areas where grouse shooting interests prevailed, access to moors was forbidden to the general public. Early this century mass trespasses were organised to draw attention to this. The most famous of the mass trespass protests were in the hills of the Peak District where the Pennine Way association was formed in 1938. The tradition is continued with the Ramblers Association 'Forbidden Britain' days, where walkers focus attention on areas where they believe people ought to have a right to walk today.

During the war the impetus for footpath preservation was lost. People were busy digging for victory: lawns became cabbage patches and farmland became part of the war effort. So we didn't complain when old pastures were ploughed and footpaths were ruined. It seemed unpatriotic to criticise those who provided our food in times of war.

Some people, including farmers, have presumed that this unofficial takeover of public paths meant a permanent closure. They think that if a path isn't used, it becomes no longer a right of way. But this is not so. A path is a path unless it is legally closed. And legal closure is a lengthy and expensive business, to which the public can object. A proposal to divert or close a path has to be open to public enquiry if anyone makes an objection.

Many paths were closed by government orders for wartime purposes. Whole areas of land were taken over for airfields and military bases. This land has still not been released for public access and you can find many areas on the map which have a black hole for footpaths. Green lines approach an old airfield from all directions . . . and suddenly stop. You join up the lines at your peril! The land may still be used as an airfield.

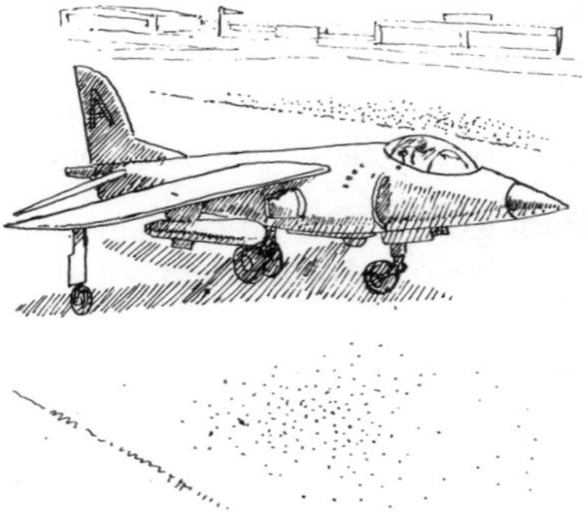

If you come across a new quarry or a recently-built reservoir the paths are likely to have been diverted around the edge, rather than closed, as attitudes to the preservation of public paths have changed for the better in recent times.

To those of us who browse over maps, loving the old ones as well as the new, and tracing the steps of our ancestors over fields and hills, the ancient routes feel like lifelines across the country. They link one church spire to another, from one hilltop landmark to the next, following a continuous line of boundary hedge, joining old green tracks, and crossing streams and rivers at ancient fording points.

It grieves us to see the ancient hedgerows being ripped out and burnt and the connecting links between paths left neglected and abandoned. We are alarmed by the encroachment on our paths of motorways, housing estates and industrial developments.

The only consolation we have is that the recent Act of Parliament has re-stated that rights of way should be left undisturbed or be made good within 14 days and kept visible on the ground. The 1990 Rights of Way Act is a massive step forward in path protection. Whether it will be more honoured in the breach than in the observance will need to be seen! But at least it has been clearly and publicly declared that farmers should leave paths clear. It is now illegal to allow crops to grow on or to encroach upon the path.

Perhaps we shall now be able to admire those 'long fields of barley and of rye, That clothe the wold and meet the sky' (Tennyson, *The Lady of Shallot*) secure in the knowledge that we won't have to force our way through them.

4.3 Footpath law

> If a traveller from afar leave the road and then neither shouts nor blows a horn, he is to be regarded as a thief, to be either killed or ransomed.
>
> Laws of Wihtraed 695 AD

As law-abiding citizens we need to be reassured about our rights and responsibilities when walking in the country.

To learn more about our rights and the farmers' responsibilities, about what we cannot do and what landowners cannot do, we have to look elsewhere in the statute books.

Trespass

A walker should not trespass. Some notices inform you that trespassers will be prosecuted. In fact, trespass is a civil wrong, not a crime and, except for trespass on operational railway lines, trespassers cannot be prosecuted unless they do damage or trespass deliberately intending to steal or commit some other crime. Even on operational railway lines, you can only be prosecuted if you refuse to leave when told to do so. Disused railway lines do not come into the same category and so only the normal rules of trespass damage apply.

In my early days of walking, older rambling friends used to say: 'There is no law of trespass, only a law of damage, so if a landowner says you're off the path, offer him six-pence to cover any damage and ask him which is the quickest way off his land to get back to the path you want.' Perhaps that is still good advice, if you make some allowance for inflation!

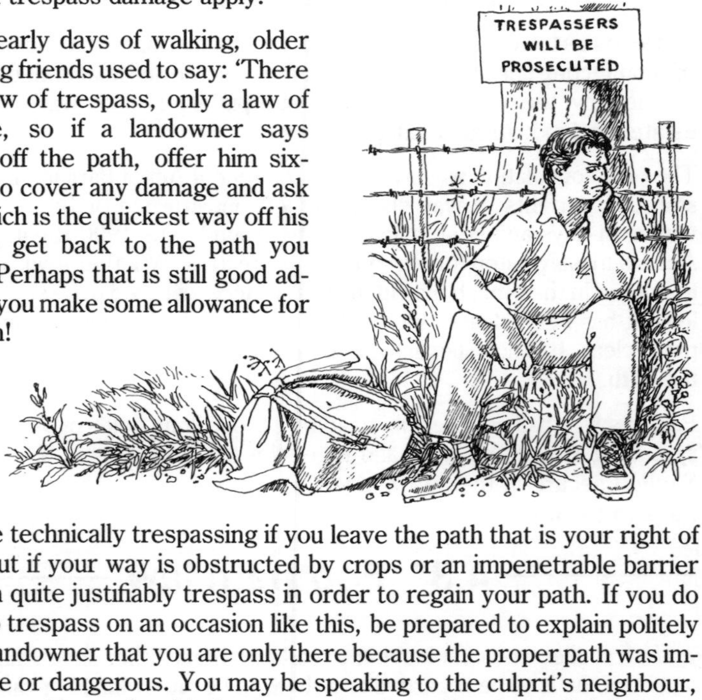

You are technically trespassing if you leave the path that is your right of way. But if your way is obstructed by crops or an impenetrable barrier you can quite justifiably trespass in order to regain your path. If you do need to trespass on an occasion like this, be prepared to explain politely to the landowner that you are only there because the proper path was impassable or dangerous. You may be speaking to the culprit's neighbour, who has nothing to do with the obstruction. I usually ask first if the right of way field belongs to them and then either apologise for my trespass from it onto their land or threaten to report their obstruction, whichever is appropriate!

Obstruction

A farmer or landowner should not obstruct a right of way. The owner of the subsoil is obliged to leave a free passage over the surface of the highway. (Just as in the deeds of a house it may be stated that the land under the adjoining road belongs to the houseowner, but that free passage must be allowed along the public road.)

The Country Code

- Enjoy the countryside and respect its life and work.
- Guard against all risk of fire.
- Fasten all gates.
- Keep your dogs under close control.
- Keep to public paths across farmland.
- Use gates and stiles to cross fences, hedges and walls.
- Leave livestock, crops and machinery alone.
- Take your litter home.
- Help to keep all water clean.
- Protect wildlife, plants and trees.
- Take special care on country roads.
- Make no unnecessary noise.

Crops

It is the duty of the Highway Authority to keep the surface of a footpath clear. It has the right to remove any crop which interferes with the highway, ie the path.

Barbed wire

Barbed wire was acknowledged to be a real problem to walkers as far back as the 1890s, when Barbed Wire Acts were passed in Parliament. The Barbed Wire Act of 1893 was designed to control the use of barbed wire for fences beside highways. The 1894 Act forbade the obstruction by barbed wire across a path. These acts are still in operation (though now subsumed under section 143 of the 1959 Highways Act, part VII and the 1980 Highway Act section 164) but I do not know of any prosecutions.

The 1980 Highway Act, section 164, gives the local authority the power to remove barbed wire and to take proceedings against the landowner who erects it near or across the highway. If the local authority happens to be the landowner, then any ratepayer in the district may take proceedings against them.

A duty of care

The owner and occupier of land has a duty of care towards visitors who have a right to be there, ie footpath walkers, providing they are not trespassing or doing anything unlawful. Local authorities have a duty to see that rights of way are kept in good condition. They are required to ensure that footpath signposts are erected on roads and that the laws are obeyed.

If you feel you are not properly cared for, you can complain to the local footpath officer at County Hall. Seriously made complaints are usually investigated and followed up. But you need to be sure of your facts and give accurate details.

Sample complaint form

Date ....
Complainant's name ....
Address ....
Tel no ....
Path number or map reference ....
Nearest village or parish ....
Name of landowner/occupier/agent if known ....
Details of problem (with explanatory sketch map) ....
....
....
....
Send to: The Rights of Way Officer
.... County Hall
....
....
....

Landowners sometimes declare that they didn't know there was a footpath across the land. There is usually no excuse for this nowadays as rights of way are described on land search forms when a house is bought or sold.

Closure of paths

People sometimes think that if a path has not been walked for 15 years it is no longer a right of way. This is not so. A right of way is a right of way and cannot be closed without the due process of law. If a landowner tells you that this particular path is closed, you can express your doubts as to the likelihood of such a closure. Even if you see an obvious crater, made by quarrying, it is most likely that the route has simply been diverted, not closed. Ask where the path goes NOW. Show your map and ask for advice as to the best and quickest way to regain your right of way. (And check later with the definitive map to see if the information was accurate and not misleading or false!)

Creation of paths

But, on the other hand, it IS true that if a path has been walked for 20 years without any objection or hindrance it can be claimed as a public right of way. This is why some landowners shut a well-used path for one day of the year, so that they can continue to claim it as a private road even though they are willing to let the public use it as a permissive path.

Permissive paths are not permanent rights of way but are only 'lent' to the public for as long as the owner thinks fit. They are not marked in green or red on OS maps.

Towpaths are not necessarily rights of way. If they have no red or green line on the map, you walk them at your own discretion unless you know that they have been walked for 20 years without any closure.

The seashore

There is no right of way along a seashore and you cannot complain if the sea comes in and covers your footsteps or ruins your boots.

River crossings

Local authorities are required to ensure that bridges are installed where footpaths cross rivers, streams and other natural water courses. (Bridges over ditches are the responsibility of the farmers and land-owners.)

If you come to a river and you cannot get across, see if there is an ancient ferry provided for transport to the other side. Some ferries go back to ancient charters whereby one local person is obliged to provide a ferry service and permitted to make a charge as part of a rental agreement. This often needs some research to find out who is now responsible for providing the ferry, but it can save a long detour along roads to reach bridges. It is most unusual for a footpath to end at a river, because historically the crossing of rivers, by bridge, ford or ferry, has always been vitally important to trade and travel.

4.4 Bulls and other beasts

There are laws to protect you from dangerous animals, so you should be able to walk with confidence that the law is on your side!

A bull is a dangerous animal

. . . and some bulls are more dangerous than others.

According to the 1981 Wildlife and Countryside Act the most dangerous ones are:

- Bulls over 10 months old. They are not allowed in footpath fields unless they are with cows or heifers. They are considered more dangerous when kept alone in a field.
- Bulls of recognised dairy breeds. Ayrshires, Friesians, Dairy Shorthorns, Guernseys, Jerseys and Kerry bulls are considered dangerous even when kept with females. They should never be in a public right of way field.
- Any bull which a farmer knows to be dangerous.

Getting to know your bulls

It is not easy to learn and to remember the distinctive features of all the recognised dairy breeds. A farming manual might provide you with illustrations of some of the best-known ones, but with the increasing popularity of rare breeds you might find it difficult to recognise them all and to classify them as dairy or beef bulls.

You could learn the distinctive features of the less dangerous Hereford or Charolais beef bulls. But you might find it more difficult to discover their age. (If the bull has a ring through its nose you can be pretty sure it has reached the age of discretion.)

My own DIY rule is that if the bull has longer legs than I have, it is likely to be a dairy bull. Do not wait to examine its pedigree and if it looks as though it could run as fast as you can, do not attempt to find out if it intends to try. It is actually safer to presume that any bull in your way is a potential threat and danger.

Never take unnecessary risks, especially if you have other people with you, and follow these guide lines:

- Avoid even the stumpiest-legged Hereford.
- Keep your distance.
- Walk round the edge of the field.
- Look out for emergency escape routes through the hedge.
- Walk through the neighbouring fields, if that's possible.
- Report the fact that you had to take evasive action because you were, quite sensibly, afraid.

To put the matter of dangerous bulls in perspective, however, I must say that I have only once been charged by a bull in 30 years of walking. It was a black and white one, with long legs. I was with a large group of people, and this may have been what disturbed and offended him. To be fair to the bull, he gave plenty of warning by bellowing loudly before charging. And everyone escaped by diving through the hedge. All this happened a long time ago and I'm pretty sure that bull is now dead. I do not know if the farmer was prosecuted; but he should have been.

Groups of animals can be frisky but heifers and bullocks are usually only high-spirited and inquisitive. They may look alarming as they approach at high speed, but they usually come to a sudden halt to avoid getting too close to strangers. Speaking to them firmly or waving your arms determinedly up and down to distract them usually stops them or drives them away.

If you have a dog with you this is likely to excite animals in fields and it may be more difficult for you to stop them following the dog. Your dog should be kept close to you, preferably on a lead, and this may give you problems if you do not like other animals in such close proximity. Dogs may not be your best friends in a pasture field.

Cows

> One day I set out with intent to trudge to Filey Bridge, but was frightened back by two cows.
>
> Charlotte Brontë Filey, June 6th 1852

Cows in a herd are peaceful animals—they usually stand and let you pass—but beware of cows with calves. Cows can be aggressive if they think their young ones are under threat. It is always wise to keep away from new calves. The mothers can be very protective and are sometimes threatening to intruders. Do not walk between a cow and her calf.

Horses

Horses can race round a field in an excitable manner and it is often difficult to know whether they are used to people and therefore excessively familiar, expecting apples and sugar lumps, or whether they are lonely or hostile or highly strung. They do not like to be looked straight in the eye, even when being patted. I tend to ignore them and walk quietly on when I am by myself.

Stallions are territorial. They mark out their territory by depositing dung round the field boundary. It might be a clever tactical move to respect their territorial boundary by keeping to the land between the dung and the hedge.

If horses are clustered around the gate or stile where you want to enter the field you can try various techniques:

- Shoo them away. (I do not like doing this, as it might frighten, excite or irritate them.)
- Wait until they get bored by your company. Sometimes if you spend time quietly near the animals on the other side of the fence, they get used to you, lose interest and wander off. (This may take some time, though, however boring you are or try to be. Horses are remarkably patient animals.)
- Wait until you get bored with their company, by which time you will have lost your initial fear. Simply walk through them, pushing past the head end and speaking calmly to them. Avoid the back leg and tail end. The tail isn't likely to do any damage, but the legs just might!
- Move away and take an alternative route if there is one. It's never good to allow yourself to be frightened, as animals seem to sense this. If you are scared, avoidance is the best tactic.

We all learn our own ways of dealing with animals but the general rule is to treat nature with respect and animals with caution.

Unless you are very confident that you know what you are doing, don't touch or interfere until you have been properly introduced. It is a good idea not to pat animals or make a fuss of them until you are safely on the other side of the fence, and only if you are sure their mother doesn't mind or their father isn't looking.

Beware of any animal alone in a field. It may have been kept separate because it is sick: and a sick animal can be unpredictable. It may be lonely and too anxious to share your company, or it may be an aggressive male.

A good rule if you see a sick animal, is to tell the nearest farmer. But if it's a lamb with its head stuck in a wire fence or a sheep upturned on its back, you might like to try out your own Herriott-country 'tender loving care' technique to rescue them. You and the sheep are not likely to do much harm to one another and even if the animal shows no gratitude, you will feel a glow of satisfaction.

If an animal does behave in a frightening manner or do any damage to you at all while you are on a footpath, report it to the police or to your footpath officer. There is a law against keeping dangerous animals in a public place or on a public footpath.

5

WALKING WITH CHILDREN

Planning walks with children in the group requires all the knowledge learnt in the preceding units, but must consider the limitations and requirements of those children.

If you experienced happy family outings when you were young, you will want to pass on these pleasures and disciplines to other young people. Late starters to walking, however, will find useful ideas and advice for introducing children of all ages to the joys of walking.

Walking and rambling is a healthy and economical pastime, but it needs planning and care to train children in the way they should go about it. Some careful attention to details can bring into line the needs of children and adults walking together.

There is no rule about when children should start walking. Here are some guidelines for each stage of a child's growing up from babyhood to adolescence. A dedicated and committed family of walkers can train a baby from the cradle to enjoy walking excursions or they can wait until the older child chooses to walk with the grown ups or with his or her own friends. Children may need encouraging at every stage, so it is essential to provide them with rucksack, boots or trainers.

Babies (0–18 months)

Few walkers take their babies on walks immediately they are born. Adults with very young babies probably have little spare energy for such pleasures as walking. Besides, even tiny babies become heavy after some time in your arms.

A baby sling provides one answer to the problem for those who are really committed to walking and who have accommodating babies. Once you can carry a sling competently, a baby need not mean the postponement of walking until they grow up.

Slings

A sling to carry the child leaves the adult's arms free for better balance and babycare. When looking for a sling, consider the size of your baby, the strength of your arm and back muscles and the width of your shoulders. It is also worth thinking about whether you would like your child on your back, out of sight, or if you would prefer to clutch your baby to your chest, where you can see what is happening and talk more easily to it.

Before you buy, look in the catalogues and baby magazines or talk to friends for the most up-to-date information on recent models.

Points to watch out for:
(a) support for the baby's head and neck;

(b) protection from cold and wet;
(c) secure but easily manipulated kinds of fastening;
(d) absence of constriction round the top of the legs;
(e) expense;
(f) ease of washing;
(g) even pressure and padding for the carrier.

Some slings are really designed for parents doing short-term activities like shopping and they may not be suitable for long distance walking because of the lack of cushioning to protect the baby from a rough ride. However, leading manufacturers of walking equipment have a range of baby slings which are more like rucksacks. The structure of the models vary from aluminium tubing which holds the bag for the baby to sit in away from the adult's body with sufficient space for some cushioning to be inserted such as spare clothing or a towel. It is important that these slings have adequate padding for the adult's shoulders and back so that the baby can be carried for a longer period. If you decide to use one for your baby, try it out on short walks. Remember that the baby has not much freedom of movement and not much field of vision when clutched closely to the body of an adult.

Rucksack seats

Babies soon grow out of slings. You might then need to consider a rucksack chair: but try one first, loaded with a big, bouncing baby. With some models it may be difficult to lift the loaded seat on to the adult's back without assistance. A baby can be carried in the backpack seat as if it were another piece of luggage; but this is not to be recommended for people with any back weakness. Both with slings and rucksack seats it is advisable to borrow (if possible) a particular model and try it out for a day to find out if it is suited to you.

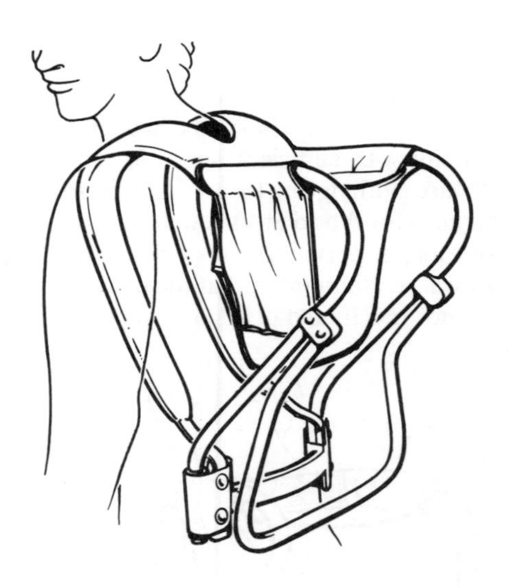

If you do not like having your baby on your back without being able to see what it is doing, make sure that a second person is able to keep an eye on the child. It is important to be aware of a child's fragility and to check constantly that its head and neck are supported.

It is easy to forget that while the adults are maintaining their body temperature through exercise, the baby, being carried inactive, can suffer from cold.

Clothing

Protect the child from the elements of cold wind, rain and sun, and regularly check the welfare of the child confined to a seat.

Baby food and equipment

Adults taking a young baby on a walk will need to adapt their normal routine. Baby food can be packed in cool bags and hot water for drinks or to warm food can be carried in vacuum flask containers. A supply of nappies, cleaning materials and plastic bags for carrying home rubbish (including disposable nappies) should be packed.

Distance

The distance you travel with a young child depends on:

- your equipment;
- the weather;
- the surface of the route;
- your stamina in carrying the extra weight of baby plus belongings;
- the baby's tolerance;
- the amount of food and drink and the number of nappies you wish to carry.

Using a push-chair to take a baby out on a walk might seem to be the next logical stage, especially as the baby grows and becomes heavier. But there are many snags to taking a push-chair. It is really a matter of personal choice whether to carry the baby in a push-chair or in a sling. A push-chair may seem the easier option but you will have to modify your planning and choice of route.

Suitable routes for push-chairs are discussed overleaf (Routes for Family Walks).

Routes for push-chairs

Footpaths are not usually suitable for walking with a push-chair, (see unit 4). Even if you choose a route with few stiles and no obstacles, the surface is often too rough. Farm lanes and tracks are the only real option, although it is advisable not to attempt too great a distance at first.

Before taking a push-chair on a walk, check the suspension because a really bumpy ride is not recommended. Meeting farm vehicles on a rough track can be very awkward because you have to pull the push-chair out of the way over rough ground. You will need to pull the chair behind you and check that the baby is strapped in (if possible see that someone walks behind you to pick up the pieces of equipment that invariably drop out of the push-chair).

Routes for Family Walks

Some especially planned routes cater for push-chairs and wheelchairs. These paths have easily negotiable handgates and cleared surfaces. Many of these are nature trails through woods and around farms where walkers can see animals and crops.

Well-maintained cycle tracks, which are often beside disused railways or canals, are suitable for push-chairs and wheelchairs. There are also well-trodden routes leaving from picnic spots, in areas of natural beauty, forest trails, farm trails or a walk on the front at the seaside.

The local county hall or information office may have lists of walks suitable for wheelchairs and push-chairs. And, there may be short, easy walks described in local publications.

A note on care on country roads

Even in towns, walking with babies or children in push-chairs is not always straightforward. Skill is needed to control the steering and brakes, to avoid sudden lurches and bumps and to allow extra time for crossing roads. Everything is much slower when you take a push-chair on a walk.

In the country these problems are magnified. There are few smooth, level pavements for pedestrians, traffic lights or pedestrian crossings. Even if there is a grass verge, it is usually far too difficult to take wheelchairs, push-chairs or prams along them. Traffic on country roads can be very fast and more dangerous than in towns. The roads wind and bend and country drivers are often unprepared to meet pedestrians and children in push-chairs.

Even a slow moving tractor can be a hazard for a push-chair on a country road where there is little room to pull in, so you need to keep your eyes and ears open all the time for oncoming danger, knowing that you need more time to negotiate your push-chair and child out of the way on a minor road.

Adults wanting suitable push-chair walks in the country might follow the sort of walks described in the preceding section (Routes for Family Walks).

— Toddlers (18 months onwards —

Toddlers, having just learnt to walk, love it. And, they are great fun to walk with! Unlike adults, toddlers go in spurts of running, stopping, looking and falling. They really need a walk tailored to them. As toddlers tire easily and suddenly, adults must modify their walking habits to allow for the child's capabilities, which means planning shorter distances and adapting to their style.

Country parks and short walks down the lane are adequate for beginners. Even walks to the playground can give useful experience of jumping, sliding and balancing, skills which will be needed when proper country walking begins! In the meantime, you may need the push-chair for the return journey, when the child has been worn out!

Clothing and equipment

When considering clothing for children who are being carried or transported in a push-chair, imagine how you would feel sitting in a deck chair moving at 3 or 4 miles per hour.

There are very good one piece garments suitable for toddlers, both for walking or for push-chair journeys. The attached hood and mitts and socks are ideal for a young child sitting still in the cold.

Take spare clothes with you for when the child falls in the mud or in puddles and pack a bag of snacks for times of stress!

Rising fives

As children grow and become stronger they love to explore. On walks they can find patches of woodland, hills to run up and different textures of sand, clay, chalk and mud soil which are very exciting to a child. You don't need to walk them very far to discover these delights. There is always something to excite a lively infant if you use your wits and eyes to find it.

Schoolchildren (5–7)

At this age children can join group walks designated as suitable for families. Your local rambling group may provide such an occasion or you may find a suitable Fungus Foray or Bat Count or some similar outing organised by a nature group (but check first to see if children would be welcome).

Five year olds, if kept sufficiently interested, can walk about five miles. They can keep up with gently paced adults without needing to be carried, especially if there are other children to set them a good example and to keep them company.

Not all children at this age want to walk so far. You have to know your child and judge what is a reasonable distance. There are several ways of encouraging a child to walk further than they think they really want to, so that they fit in with the whole group.

Many parents try:

(a) prizes for such things as being the first to see the next waymark sign or collecting the most different grasses, or for completing the walk
(b) games of imagination such as you're a mountain pony . . . an explorer . . . a great big giant . . .
(c) treasure hunts; ie, see what is round the next corner or over the next hill
(d) word games like 'I spy' (G for gran and goosegrass and grass-hopper . . .)
(e) races (First to the top or First to find a mole hill or something blue . . . or something to feed to a hamster . . .)
(f) praise (What a good walker you are! Come to the front and help carry the map or compass or torch . . .)
(g) treats (chocolate, nuts, fruit)
(h) singing (nursery rhymes, counting songs and hymns, are to be recommended as they have rousing rhythms and memorable words!)
(i) story telling; especially good if you have to wait for transport or are on the journey home. You can also adapt your normal indoor or travelling games.

All these distractions can be useful at times. You have to choose which is appropriate for your children on particular occasions. Many of them have the added advantage of helping a child's language development while opening their eyes to the joys of the countryside.

Food

Children soon burn up calories. They may not eat large meals, but need quick energy-giving food and drink at regular, short intervals. They need frequent encouragement in the shape of food and drink and a lot of sit-downs between climbs! Sandwiches can be opened half an hour after setting off and divided into portions to be eaten every quarter of an hour when the going gets tough!

Clothes and equipment

Proper walking boots are not an option for most children, as their feet grow so fast. . . . Wellies or strong shoes are the best most parents can afford. For very short walks they can manage in canvas shoes, but this creates a dilemma for adults. If they are lightly shod, do you wear your good strong walking gear, so that you can beat down nettles and carry children over wet patches or do you wear shoes and clothing similar to theirs, so that you can experience and sympathise with how they feel when faced with rough ground or sharp thistles?

It is advisable to provide children with the most suitable gear you can find and tailor the activity to their size and strength. Walking should be enjoyed and children can be put off it for ever if they don't feel adequately kitted out.

— Children's groups (8–early teens) —

For children in this age group there are clubs such as cubs and brownies, summer playgroups, and activity holiday playschemes, which provide activities with other children, such as organised walks with qualified adults. It is important for the growing child to experience peer group activities in the country under adult supervision and in such groups, your children can enjoy some independence.

As children grow they may go for day walks, camp fires and even nights away from home. There may be treasure hunts and orientation games and trail-laying and waymark-following games. They will soon learn to prepare their own gear for a walk.

Teenagers may choose to go off in peer groups, ideally with a responsible leader who will discuss equipment, food and clothing and safety rules.

Later they may want to go off on their own, and do schemes like the Duke of Edinburgh award or a Venture Scout badge. Sponsored walks and activity holidays might tempt young people to walk without adult supervision.

If children have done a lot of family walking, they will know what to wear and what to take.

If they are planning a walking holiday, it is a good idea for them to test out some day walks first; or try walking holidays specially designed for young people (see the list of addresses for YHA and HF holiday weeks for young people). Youth Hostelling is a good start for holidays independent of an adult.

All children are to be encouraged in self reliance. Let them learn to provide for themselves as soon as they can. They know what they like to eat and drink and wear and if they want to rebel against your choice, they will learn for themselves what is most sensible. By the time they get to Youth Hostelling on their own they should be able to plan their own routes, provide their own food, pack their own gear sensibly and navigate.

Once children are educated to respect life in the country and understand walking rules, they can enjoy their walks safely without adult supervision.

6 KEEPING A RECORD

You may be one of those people who carry long-lasting visual memories in your head and do not need a picture or photograph to remind you of what you saw. But you may, like me, be one who sees again or sees for the first time when you look at the visual record.

— 6.1 Photographs and sketches —

Your own sketches or snapshots of walks may serve as a useful factual record for you. (At one time I took pictures of bulls so that I could use them as evidence of a dangerous footpath. Later I took photographs of difficult stiles and crossing places, with friends perched precariously in impossible positions.)

Your pictures may give you inestimable pleasure, bringing back scenes you might otherwise have lost. Your photograph album, like your journal, does not have to be for others. Your snaps do not have to be particularly beautiful. They may centre around your special interest, or they may include a miscellany of items that took your fancy: odd objects seen on walks; the psychedelic Mini parked in the farmyard on the Yorkshire moors; the steam tractor you encountered on the road to Peatling

Parva; the fox, the deer, the wallaby on the Roaches; the little house where you had tea; the big bull that didn't chase you; the cowslips, the old barn, the tractor, the little bridge, the field of blue flax or golden barley waving in the wind . . .

One picture might bring back vividly to you the whole memory of a day's walk or a week's holiday.

Keeping a record is not, of course, obligatory! Memories have a way of resurfacing without any effort on your part. You can be reminded by friends' conversation or a return visit; a familiar feel or smell.

6.2 Writing a diary

You do not need any literary talent to keep a diary. All you need is pen and paper. I am an inveterate diary writer: I keep journals of all sorts. My walking diary began as a strictly factual record of where I went, when, with whom, how many miles walked and what the weather was like. It was written in a little unlined notebook given me by my daughter nearly 20 years ago. Over the years it has extended into two other (equally small) notebooks and the content has expanded slightly to include more details of things I have found interesting.

For me it has become a rounding off of the day's walking to sit after a meal and a bath or hot shower, with my map open before me as I retrace the route and write about it in the glow of the evening.

No doubt the people I walked with would have very different memories of those days and would have noted other items.

I hope the following excerpts give an idea in a simple and vivid way of the sort of joys and excitement there are to be found in country walking.

Walking in Leicestershire: A case study

Most of the walks described in my diary took place in Leicestershire and Rutland, but I hope that the examples are of general interest. I have chosen pieces to illustrate features already mentioned elsewhere in the book or aspects I felt deserved a mention of some sort.

The condition of our paths is as varied as you will find anywhere. We have our own 100-mile Long Distance Path, the Leicestershire Round; many overgrown, neglected and thoroughly obstructed paths; and the vast reservoir of Rutland Water which has drowned many others!

I have kept the place names, because they have a charm of their own, but hope you will read this very personal and localised evidence as a general indication of what you might find when you walk elsewhere in Britain in any season of the year.

Here is, in fact, a microcosm of English country walking!

From the diary of a (town dwelling) country walker

1977 *Jan 1st* Frosty morning but the ice wasn't too bad. Walked over frozen ruts in fields. Frozen nose and toes and finger tips at first. Missing footbridge at Brooke, missing since 1922!

Jan 23rd Took 12 students on the same walk as yesterday, but avoided the worst of the mud at Hungarton by trespassing along to the second footbridge. There's snow still by the hedges. Students threw snowballs with great hilarity. Lots of birds (fieldfare?) and bluetits in hedges but no lambs or wild animals. Quite mild. We stopped in little cemetery for tea from thermos. Gravestones there all date from 1720-ish. Isolated from village. I wonder why?

Feb 19th Lovely sunny day, blue skies, snowdrops. Spring, after a terribly wet yesterday! Very muddy through the gates, but otherwise not bad underfoot. Good views over Rutland Water. It's now finished and full, and Hambleton appears as an island in the middle. I was surprised that it was so close to Oakham: at Egleton it only seemed one field away. Several roads and footpaths on my map are now dead ends into water!

June 4th Old Salt Way a quiet and interesting old road. We sunbathed on the grass verge at one point, among the cow parsley. Still, I'd rather go over fields.

1978 *June 6th* Walking alone is different. You notice more. Saw hares and pheasants and kestrels. I don't usually feel lonely. Often think more, of how odd life is and who would have thought things would turn out like this.

Nov 25th Frost overnight, sun in morning, rain, hail, sleet, snow, cold wind. 14 miles and a lot of obstructing ditches and barbed wire. Lovely when it was over. Great fun really. There were 14 of us and swans on the river in snow at Ratcliffe Culey.

1979 *Jan 20th* Slushy deep snow. Wore wellies. Not really cold. Interesting to see all the bird tracks in the snow, laid out as if by convict marks on a bicycle tyre. Hare and fox marks, too. Snipe flying.

April 19th South Croxton. A man and his wife planting trees next to New Covert. Mixed beech, oak, larch, etc. How lovely! In 15 years I'll be able to remember I was there on the day it was planted. It's netted round to keep out rabbits. New Covert is still pretty impenetrable. Beds of violets look really beautiful.

Sept 19th Farmer at Carlton lent me his stick to knock down nettles and told me I could leave it at other end of his property.

Dec 8th Another nice day: but a bit of a rush to do 7 miles before dark. Saw beagles hunt (on foot in brick red velvet jackets, white breeches and jockey hats) near Arnesby.

1980 *Feb 16th* Belton in Rutland. Bit drizzly at first. Saw hunters arriving at Wardley Wood—all very posh—black top hats and fearfully lordly. Then at Hallaton saw the Beaglers (Bassett hounds, on foot). One huntsman (in ginger velvet jacket, jockey cap and running shoes and whip) fell and rolled over at our feet. Didn't do his white trousers much good! Runaway riderless horse on A47 at Allexton. We slowed down the traffic while MW did a flying leap and caught the reins. What a hero! Woman in black, with veil, sitting side saddle rode up to take the animal home, with gracious thanks to us all.

May 24th Fox watching rabbits near Twyford (Quarry). Landlord at Barsby told us about the Moot stone, called Muddy stone by locals, on Ridgmeer Lane and the Old Stump cross at Ashby Pastures in wood.

July 9th JG found huge horse mushroom. Safe to eat, dark gills, peelable, fresh, smelling good and not growing under trees and not yellowing at base. There are 99 edible varieties . . . but has he got the 100th? (He ate it and didn't die.)

Aug 9th Stopped by gamekeeper on Garendon estate, saying it was a private road. (Possibly true . . . but he let us through, as we were reasonably polite, sufficiently knowledgeable, moderately obsequious and pretty determined!!)

1981 *Sept 2nd* Lots of harvesting . . . roly poly haystacks. Combine harvesters, burnt fields and smoke . . . but all quite pleasant really. A farmer waved!

1982 *July 5th* Solo to Bardon Hill. The quarry has already expanded a lot since I last went. Not a bad day. A partridge, a pheasant, several rabbits and a lot of wild flowers. Are there more varieties around this year or do I imagine that the meadows are more colourful? Perhaps farmers are spraying less, since all the outcry against insecticides? And perhaps the price of chemicals has gone up?

1984 *May 5th* Talked to a nice farmer at The Manor farm. He hadn't heard the farmers' programme at 7am, so I told him about it: organic farming and moves to decrease pollution, stubble burning and use of chemicals. He agreed it would be good idea.

June 9th With HF group. Two of them were over 75! and one talked all the way, naming all the plants: white briony (mandrake), heartsease, meadow plaintain, hardiron, lesser stitchwort, greater celandine, angelica . . . and told us about the cuckoos we saw. The male 'cuckoos' to call the female. She flies low; he flies high. And we saw them doing just that!

June 23rd Martinshaw woods. Ragged Robin: apparently rare now and are not the other name for herb Robert. They're like a red campion in flower only ragged and spikey-leaved.

1985 *May 24th* Rape was at the walkable stage, covering us in yellow pollen dust up to chest height. We made a stepping stone bridge to cross the stream at Claybrook Magna mill.

May 26th 6 pm. I walked all the way round Hambleton peninsula. Surely the prettiest walk in Rutland. And to think I signed a petition against the drowning of the land here to make a reservoir. Hambleton Old Hall remains beside the water. A footpath goes uphill opposite it. It used to come across from Edith Weston. There are lots of paths under that water.

June 8th TG and I wore shorts but I walked at back (old age has low cunning!) so didn't get my knees wet from crops: he walked at front and got his all wet and cut and scratched.

1986 *Jan 1st* Frosty ground and misty air. Frozen mud much easier to walk on than squelchy mud, so we walked the 10 miles quite briskly. Picnicked in barn at Temple Mill. (The couple there have a 'Nuclear free zone' sticker on their door and invited us to use their outside loo if we wanted! Corn in Egypt in that area!) Obstructions everywhere: barbed wire, ditches, impenetrable hedges and the shoot syndicate manager tried to tell us the footpath had been moved. (He's wrong of course. It hasn't!)

April 19th We had to walk along the river bank to Cottesmore Bridge because there's still no FB over the river. From Langham Place, I walked the old route while K and S walked the new diverted route. Mine was prettier and ten minutes quicker.

Sept 27th To Packington. Three of us. Thoroughly enjoyable 12 miles. We laughed a lot and walked a very varied route: pasture, plough, horses, cattle, little mining towns, subsidence lakes with bullrushes and swans, green lanes and a nice little bit of trespass along the old canal at Overseal. Walked over the underground mine fire at Oakthorpe, where the paths are still sealed off. Giant bricks at Measham, red painted pub at Oakthorpe, crescent of houses now flattened by subsidence at Moira, new nature trail at old Moira furnace and a road not marked on the map.

Nov 29th Blackbrook reservoir. Climbers on the rocks. Road to Fenny Mill. L13 no headlands, old railway line, L15 well-walked but no way through hedge so people have reverted to the pre-diverted path, near the footbridge. L104 well-marked but no planks over ditches. Back over L14: no headland from reservoir.

We trespassed from Poachers Corner along Strawberry Hill Lane, which I believe must really be a county road, though it's marked as Private road. Shooting party at the Hermitage, just finished day's shoot on Sharpley. Leader came forward to challenge me. I asked if he was the farmer we wanted to see about the ploughed diversion headlands. That took him back a bit, so we proceeded past another dozen or so, loading birds into their van. One young man was banging a bird's head on a stone, as it wasn't dead. It looked awfully cruel to me but, cowardly, I said nothing. One act of bravery is as much as I can manage in a day. Back 3.30 just as the sun disappeared. Thick fog took over.

1987 *July 13th* Solo. Evening. Quorn . . . very pretty. Interesting architecture. The footpaths are slabbed and cobbled across the fields to the river. There are setts along riverside. Well-walked towpath with proper stiles. What a joy! 4 miles in 1½ hours.

August 25th Derbyshire. 12 miles very varied scenery. Stanton Moor, Nine Ladies stone circle (Bronze Age?). Trout under bridge at Raper Lodge jumped up to catch the crumbs M threw to them.

1988 *Feb 6th* From Castle Donington, with parish council group to investigate complaints near Hemington and Lockington. Really pretty over Daleacre (pronounced Dalager by locals). Two rampant horses that they have complained about. We managed OK, but I see what they mean.

Aug 6th Burton Lazars. Very very hot day. Crops harvested but farmer warned of paraquat on stubble, directed me incorrectly and gave wildly inaccurate (?) facts about leper burial ground, where nothing would grow. One stinking cesspit of a stream, black and horrible. No waymark signs or footpath signs. But little Dalby is so gorgeous. Kestrel sitting on buttress while I ate my sandwiches. Return from Burrough hill via nice green lanes.

1989 *Jan 29th* Noted on G's new Pathfinder map that the B90A is omitted. It's marked on mine. (That was why she hadn't been able to work out a circular 8-mile route.) Must ring County Hall to find out why this county road has been omitted by OS.

May 23rd Cold Newton and Lowesby. Lost villages, mare's tail grasses. Hollow tree with nails inside. Verger showed us badger sett under church now blocked off to keep badger out of foundations.

July 15th Castle Bytham. Lunch in pub garden. We didn't go down to the motte castle but did admire it from distance. Trespassed along the railway to avoid rape field. Took it in turns to lead through the next lot of rape, growing over the track. Watched 6 deer leaping through the ripe barley near Stocken Wood.

1990 *Feb 10th* From Cold Overton in sleet and bitter driving rain to Knossington (by which time we were wet through) past Bleak House(!) to Ladywood Lodge, where the clouds lifted and the rain stopped. Down to Langham, where the pubs welcomed us . . . even told us to leave our boots on, but we took them off and left them outside, upside down to dry off. Spread our wet garments in front of the log fire. After lunch, up to Ranksborough, where everyone collected to hear about Simon of Langham, 14th century archbishop, contemporary with Chaucer and in line for Pope, donated great treasures to Westminster Abbey. (Local Poor Boy Makes Good!)

April 16th Solo from Cossington Mill via the proposed diversions for quarrying and on to Sileby Mill. Lovely river, wide and clear as glass. About 20 swans in field near Sileby mill. Ladysmock in the meadows, marsh marigolds in the spinney.

June 30th Ratcliffe on Soar. Fine monuments in church. Blue skies, wild flowers, rabbits and squirrels running right across our path from woods into the corn and back. Met old farmer at Cuckoo Bush farm, pleased to chat, lamenting BSC (mad cow disease). He's never fed animal feed to cattle (herbivores aren't carnivores, his dad used to say). Told us the tumulus in the woods was where the cuckoos were fenced in Cuckoo Bush. (What did he mean?) The tumulus is probably Bronze Age burial chamber.

Aug 15th Marefield. Saw a badger walloping across disused railway line and down the bank.

Dec 1st At Shawell I left the group so I could walk up lovely sunken track to the old church and 12th century castle mound. Read notice about Georgian Hall being on older site, lived in by a 16th century MP called Edward Leigh. All fascinating stuff! And Tennyson wrote part of *In Memoriam* here. (The best part of the walk for me. I like exploring and finding interesting titbits.)

1991 *April 16th* At Tilton, saw fox and new ponds near the top of the hill (marked on map as springs). New ponds the flavour of the year. Quite large ones being constructed everywhere (for fishing, etc). Old dew ponds have disappeared.

May 2nd Kirby Bellars. The old gravel pits are now waterparks. Exciting green causeway path across the water to Asfordby (local pronunciation 'Assaby').

June 19th Roman road to Glooston, with the wildlife group. Rescued two sheep, one on its back (L rolled it over), one trailing barbed wire caught up in its fleece (he and M extracted it).

7

GOING FURTHER AFIELD

7.1 Long Distance Paths

These are the equivalent of motorways in our footpath system, made for long treks and heavy loads across country, away from towns and cities. The first Long Distance Paths (LDPs) were originally designed as challenge routes for walkers wishing to cover long distances, carrying their own survival equipment, through bleak or wild upland areas. They are now signposted, waymarked and maintained routes, known by name and easily accessible to the general public.

The Pennine Way, the first to be established and still perhaps the most widely-known, is one of the most strenuous. It was created, after thirty years of protest, struggle and conflict between walkers and game-keepers whose landowners and paymasters were hostile to the idea of any public access across grouse moors. When it was finally opened in 1965, it cleared a way through the moorland hills for walkers and has proved a remarkably popular trail, considering the character of much of the terrain.

The hilly backbone of England can be a very bleak place and the route is not to be recommended to beginners! Wainwright describes the Black Hill section near Bleaklow, which is a 'a beast in bad weather', as 'a brute in any weather'! The 250-mile route from Edale to Kirk Yetholme takes between 14 and 21 days to complete (and years of boasting about it afterwards!)

Not all the paths are as strenuous or as challenging as this, however. There is now a wide selection of 200 or more long distance paths well-established all over the country and you can choose the kind that suits your need.

The acorn symbol in England and the thistle symbol in Scotland mark long green trails around the coastlines, across the country from coast to coast, along the tops of most of our mountain ranges, on disused railways, beside canals and rivers. Some follow our ancient ridgeways, some trace the visible remains of old defensive walls and earthen embankment boundaries, some use hollow way tracks, drove roads and packhorse routes.

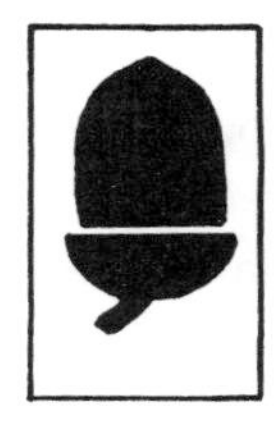

You can choose the area of the country you want to walk, the kind of path you want, and the distance you want to tackle. You can also choose whether you wish to do it the hard way or in comparative comfort!

Many people like the idea of the challenge of completing the whole of a designated way in a week or fortnight's holiday, planning their transport to the start and finish (with a celebration welcoming party at the end!) and camping or stopping in bed and breakfast accommodation on the way.

Many more are attracted by the possibility of doing a LDP walk without having to carry their equipment or camp out in the open or walk extra miles off the route to find a place to sleep: and there is now quite an industry built around the walking of long distance paths.

The Sunday papers carry many adverts for holiday operators who carry your luggage and provide transport at the end of the day's walk to a comfortable night's accommodation. Even organisations like the Youth Hostel Association provide leaders and transport for walking tours like this.

Purists may scorn, but if carrying your possessions on your back and sleeping on the hard ground are the only things that deter you from trying a long walk, you might like to indulge in a little cossetting of this kind.

You do not, however, need to complete Long Distance Paths as a marathon. You can try them in small doses. In fact you would be wise to sample any of the paths (but particularly the tough routes, of course) in small sections before you tackle the whole route, to make sure you appreciate the terrain and have the right equipment and clothing for a long distance path.

I myself am not a great LDP challenge walker. I tend to sample bits of any I come across and then choose only the most attractive parts. Thus for **Offa's Dyke** and **Hadrian's Wall**, I walk the middle bits and avoid the town stretches at either end. It is possible to centre your stay on Knighton in the heart of the most beautiful parts of **Offa's Dyke** and 'kangaroo hop' your way along the route in either direction: a suggestion that might be anathema to dedicated long distance path fanatics, who would hate the idea of messing about with a logical linear path, but it is a method which I find very satisfactory.

To walk the most interesting parts of **Hadrian's Wall** you can choose one of the lovely little towns like Corbridge or Hexham as your centre and use the regular local bus service which runs continuously in the tourist season to and fro along the road parallel to the Wall. You can start from a car park, walk along the Wall and return by bus to the car park. Next day you can choose a car park further along the Wall and walk another length and return again by bus!

Small stretches of long distance paths make quite good introductions to walking for beginners because the paths are usually so easy to follow. It is reassuring to walk a well-marked and maintained path, knowing that the route has actually been chosen for some reason by someone and that hundreds of others will have tried and tested it.

Choose your LDP with care. They vary tremendously in character. Paths like the **Cambrian Way** in Gwynedd and the **Southern Upland Way** in Scotland, for instance, are strictly for the heavy brigade! (My Scottish landlord used to say to me each morning as I set off to walk a stretch of the **Southern Upland Way**, 'Aye, it's no weather for the hills this day. Ye'd better be along the coastal path.') If you are not a dedicated, experienced and well-equipped mountain or hill walker you are advised to avoid the risks of a tough route, particularly in poor weather.

Even those routes which are near neighbours can have a very different level of difficulty. The **West Highland Way** in Scotland is a much more manageable route than the **Southern Upland Way**, although it is a little further north. The **West Highland Way**, 95 miles (153km) from Glasgow to Fort William, goes parallel with rail and road, for much of its distance, on a surface of old drove roads and tracks with stopping places not too far apart. (There are, however, some tough sections and the guide book warns you away from these.)

The **Southern Upland Way** goes 212 miles (342km) from Portpatrick on the west coast to Cockburnspath near St Abbs Head on the east coast of Scotland and is 'a big route in more ways than one'. The official guide book describes it as traversing 'some particularly hard and gruelling stretches of countryside'. It takes a route across hills, 'across the grain of the country', away from the lines of communication in the valleys, 'threading its way through areas where population is sparse and transport and shelter practically non-existent'. It is true that in certain sections you need to walk 24 or 27 miles to reach any sort of road and rescue, and some of the terrain is bleak and the weather in Scotland can sometimes be harsh: but the difficulties are described with such relish that I sometimes wonder whether the authors of Scottish LDP guide books are deliberately trying to deter people from walking their hills!

The **Cleveland Way**, which goes 93 miles (150km) round the edge of the North Yorkshire Moors and is considered to be quite a demanding challenge walk, is not such a rough, tough experience as the much shorter **Lyke Wake Walk**, which goes across the same bleak moorland. The 40-mile (65-km) **Lyke Wake Walk** should be done in 24 hours, just to make it more challenging! (Strictly not for beginners or those travelling alone!)

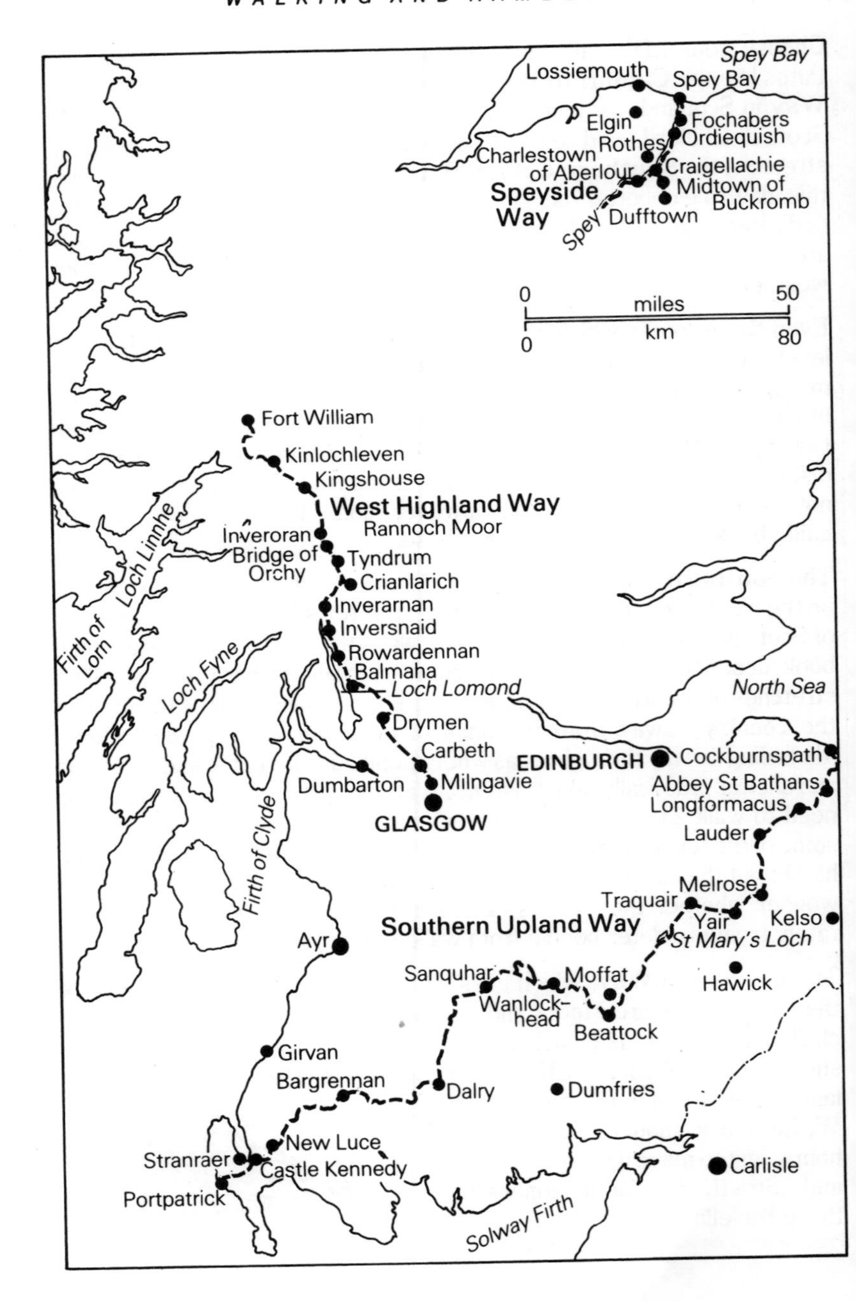
Spey Bay
Lossiemouth
Spey Bay
Elgin
Fochabers
Rothes
Ordiequish
Charlestown
of Aberlour
Craigellachie
Midtown of
Buckromb
Speyside
Way
Spey
Dufftown
0
miles
50
km
0
80
Fort William
Kinlochleven
Kingshouse
West Highland Way
Rannoch Moor
Inveroran
Bridge of
Orchy
Tyndrum
Crianlarich
Inverarnan
Inversnaid
Rowardennan
Balmaha
Loch Lomond
Drymen
Carbeth
Milngavie
Dumbarton
GLASGOW
Loch Linnhe
Firth of
Lorn
Loch Fyne
Firth of Clyde
North Sea
EDINBURGH
Cockburnspath
Abbey St Bathans
Longformacus
Lauder
Melrose
Traquair
Yair
Kelso
Southern Upland Way
St Mary's Loch
Ayr
Sanquhar
Moffat
Hawick
Wanlock-
head
Beattock
Girvan
Bargrennan
Dalry
Dumfries
New Luce
Stranraer
Castle Kennedy
Carlisle
Portpatrick
Solway Firth

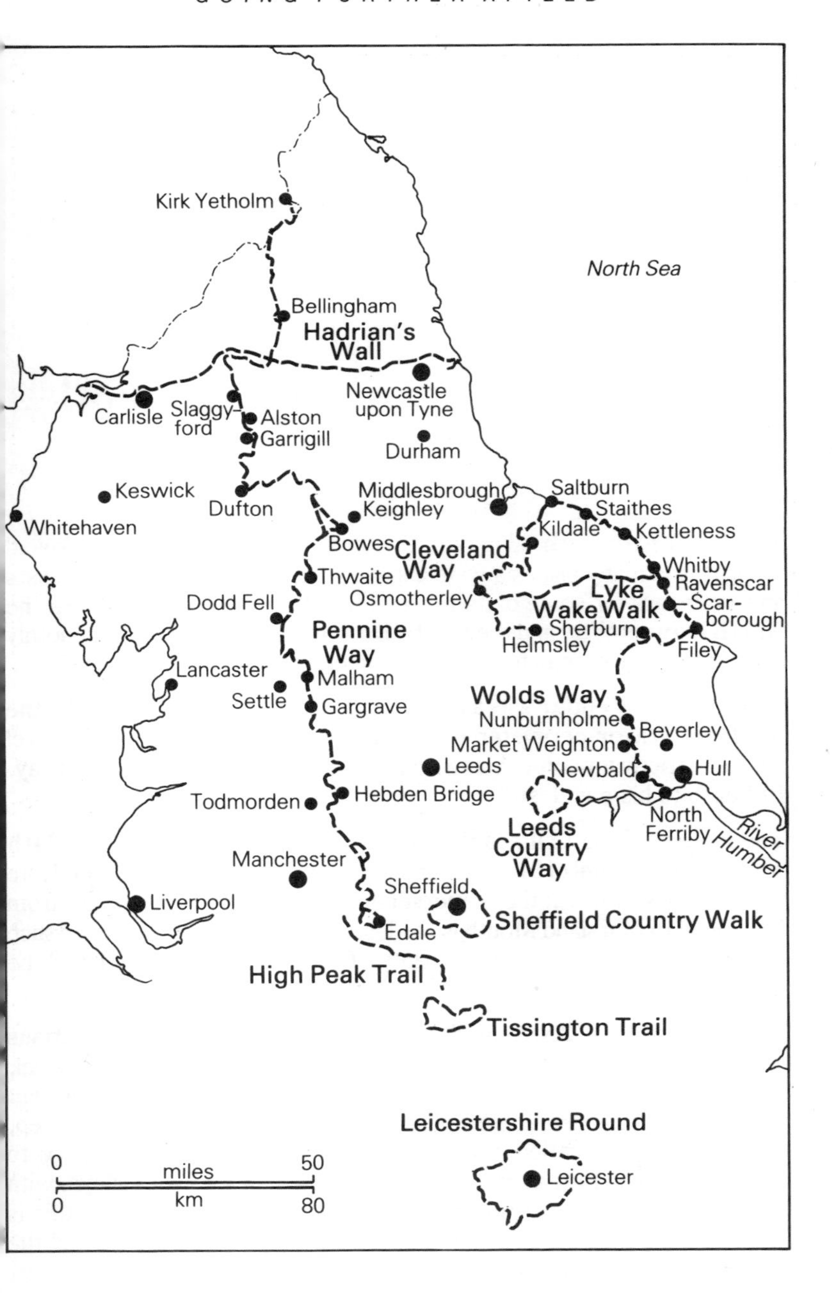
Kirk Yetholm
North Sea
Bellingham
Hadrian's Wall
Newcastle upon Tyne
Carlisle
Slaggyford
Alston
Garrigill
Durham
Keswick
Dufton
Middlesbrough
Saltburn
Staithes
Kettleness
Whitehaven
Keighley
Kildale
Bowes
Cleveland Way
Whitby
Ravenscar
Thwaite
Osmotherley
Lyke Wake Walk
Scarborough
Dodd Fell
Pennine Way
Sherburn
Helmsley
Filey
Lancaster
Malham
Settle
Gargrave
Wolds Way
Nunburnholme
Beverley
Market Weighton
Leeds
Newbald
Hull
Todmorden
Hebden Bridge
North Ferriby
River Humber
Leeds Country Way
Manchester
Sheffield
Liverpool
Sheffield Country Walk
Edale
High Peak Trail
Tissington Trail
Leicestershire Round
Leicester
0
miles
50
0
km
80

Not all of the named long distance paths are challenge walks. Some are very gentle recreational paths. There are paths like the **High Peak Trail** and the **Tissington Trail** in Derbyshire which follow old railway routes. These are often level and flat, even in high and hilly countryside, and they attract many family groups and cyclists on hired bikes out for a quiet Sunday jaunt.

The **Ridgeway Path**, along the Chilterns, follows the ancient Icknield Way. It is in many places a wide and easy track open to horses, cyclists and even cars for some of its route. Two other ridgeway paths are the **North Downs Way** and the **South Downs Way**. Both follow smoothly rounded hills, with much of the walking on springy turf.

Paths like the **Peddar's Way** in Norfolk and recreational paths like the **Rutland Water** perimeter route might seem a doddle of easy, level tracks, 'strictly for softies', as a real long distance path walker might say. But each to his own taste!

The longest of the LDPs is the **South West Peninsula Coast Path** which covers a total of 518 miles (833km), though it is usually divided into four sections of which the Somerset and Devon North Coast Path from Minehead to Marsland Mouth is the least arduous. Obviously, over such a long distance, a very great variety of scenery and conditions will be encountered.

There are at least 200 long distance paths to choose from, of various lengths, linear or circular, coastal or inland, cross country or regional, tough or easy. When you read about any LDP look for the significant words which describe it. Words like: 'challenging, rough, bleak, steep, arduous or pretty varied' and phrases like: 'in rolling countryside, with many items of historic interest, on gentle tracks, along river valleys, with many changes of level' can be very revealing. Choose whether this is what you want. Look for the distance between stopping places and the distance from escape routes.

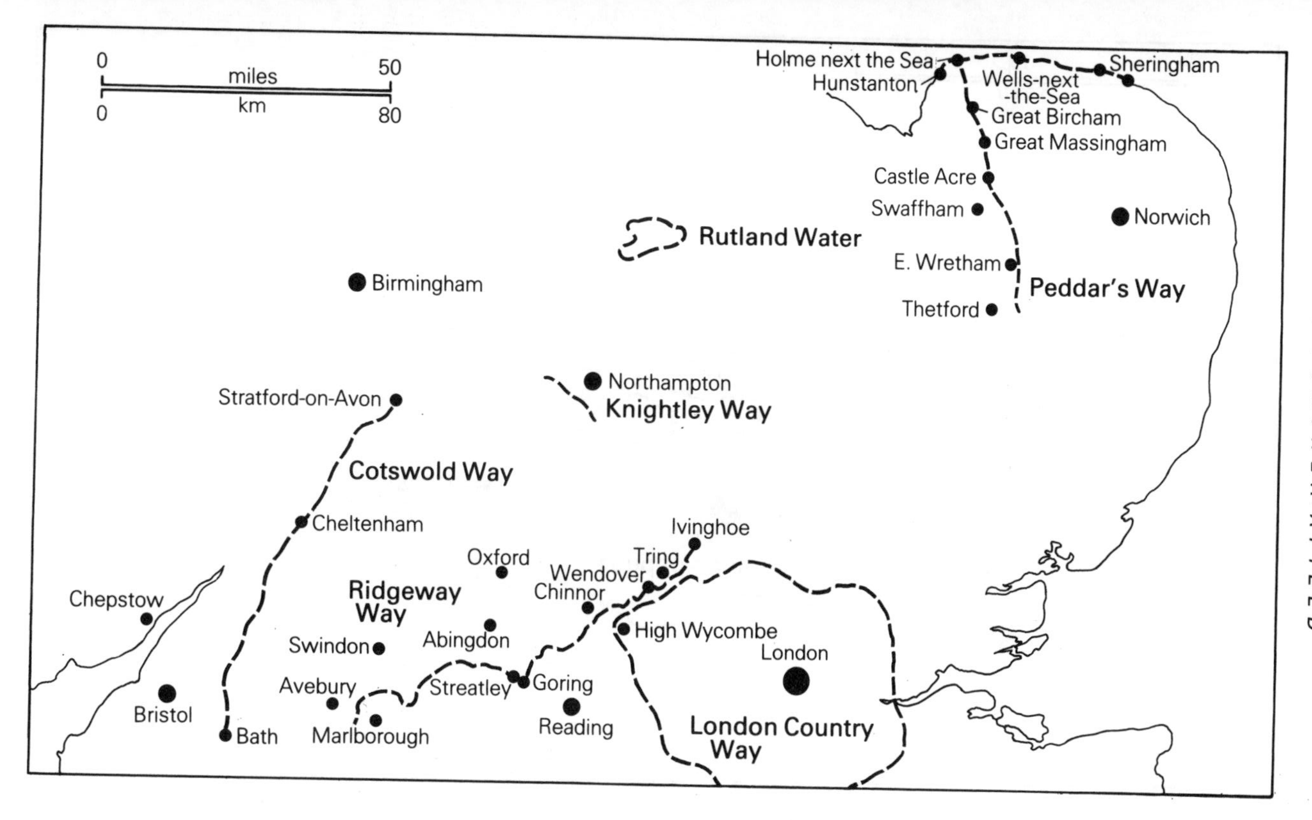

miles
km
0
50
0
80
Holme next the Sea
Hunstanton
Wells-next-the-Sea
Sheringham
Great Bircham
Great Massingham
Castle Acre
Swaffham
Norwich
Rutland Water
E. Wretham
Birmingham
Peddar's Way
Thetford
Northampton
Knightley Way
Stratford-on-Avon
Cotswold Way
Cheltenham
Ivinghoe
Oxford
Tring
Wendover
Chinnor
Ridgeway Way
Chepstow
High Wycombe
London
Abingdon
Swindon
Avebury
Streatley
Goring
Reading
Bristol
Bath
Marlborough
London Country Way

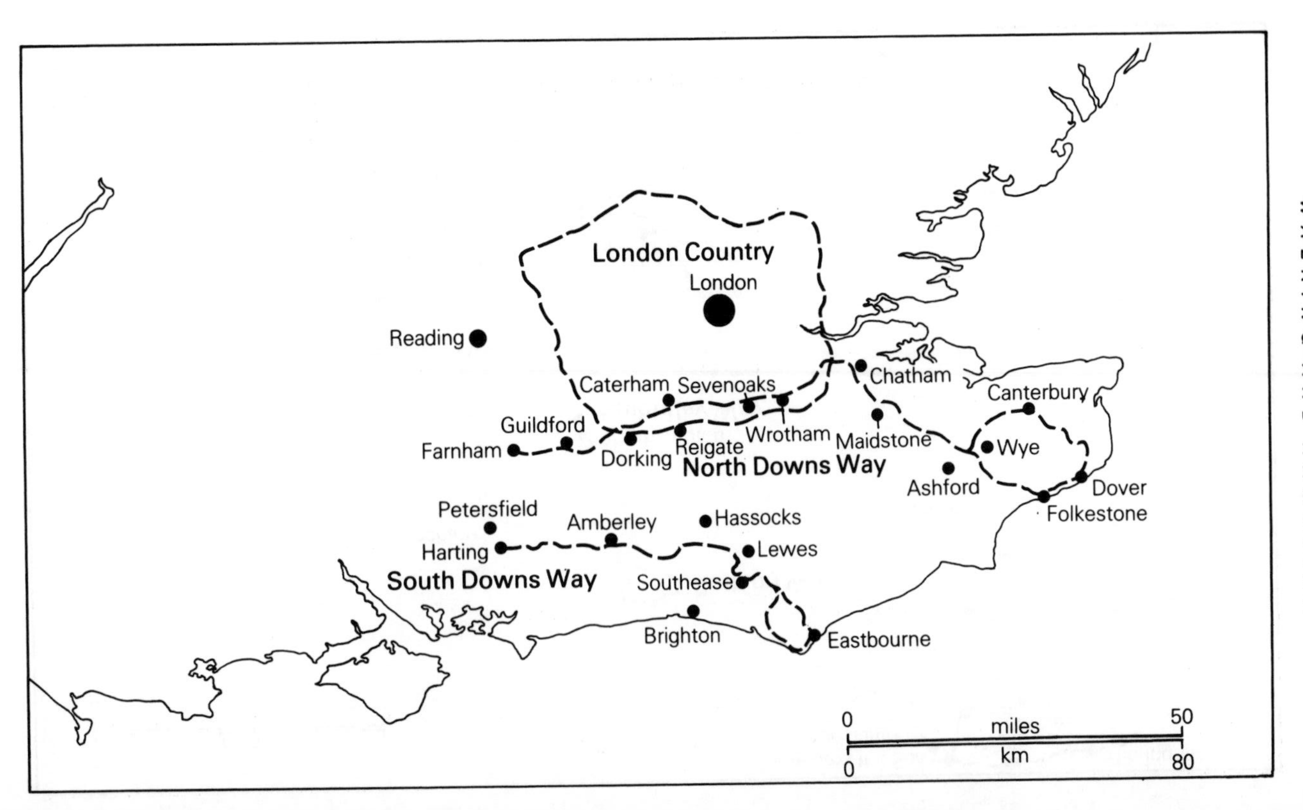
London Country
London
Reading
Chatham
Canterbury
Caterham
Sevenoaks
Guildford
Farnham
Dorking
Reigate
Wrotham
Maidstone
Wye
North Downs Way
Ashford
Dover
Folkestone
Petersfield
Amberley
Hassocks
Lewes
Harting
South Downs Way
Southease
Brighton
Eastbourne
0
miles
50
0
km
80

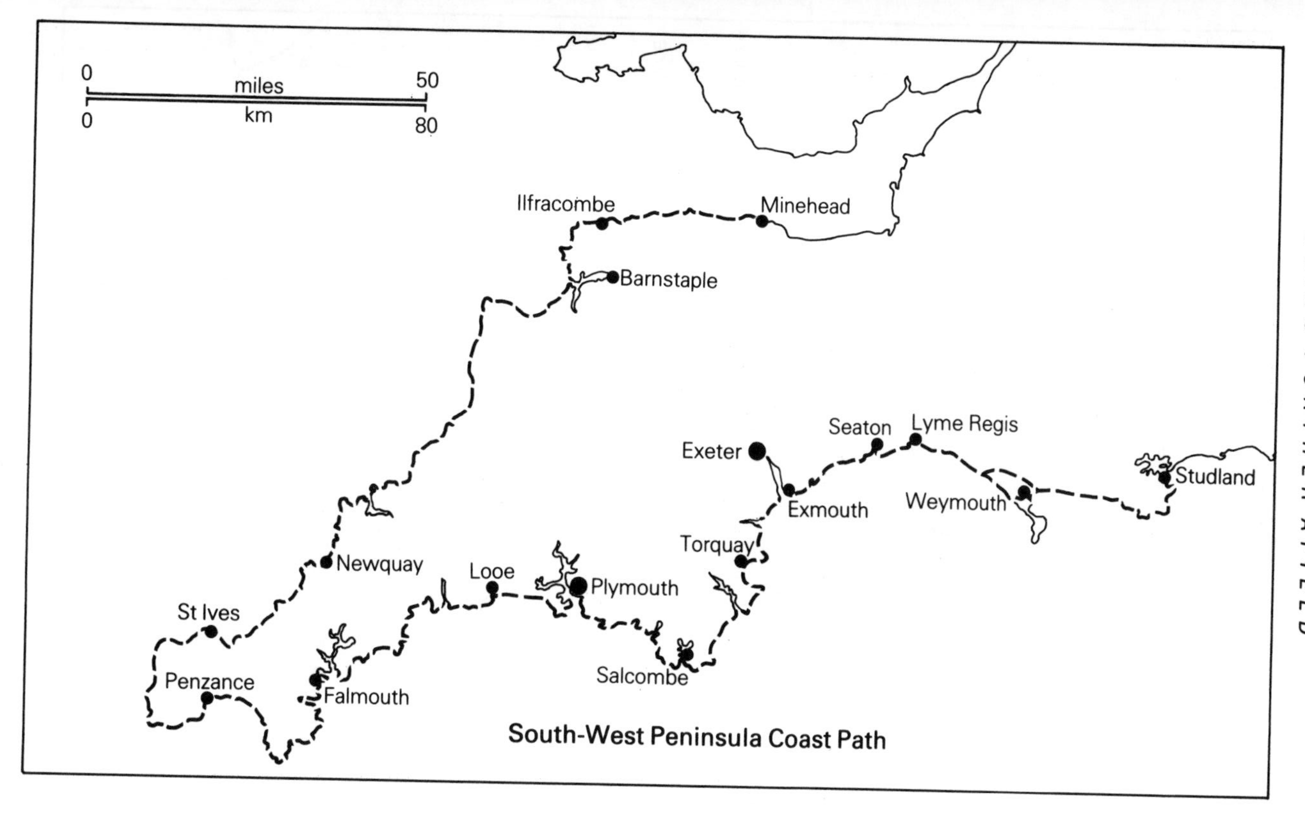

0
miles
50
0
km
80
Ilfracombe
Minehead
Barnstaple
Exeter
Seaton
Lyme Regis
Studland
Exmouth
Weymouth
Torquay
Newquay
Looe
Plymouth
St Ives
Salcombe
Penzance
Falmouth
South-West Peninsula Coast Path

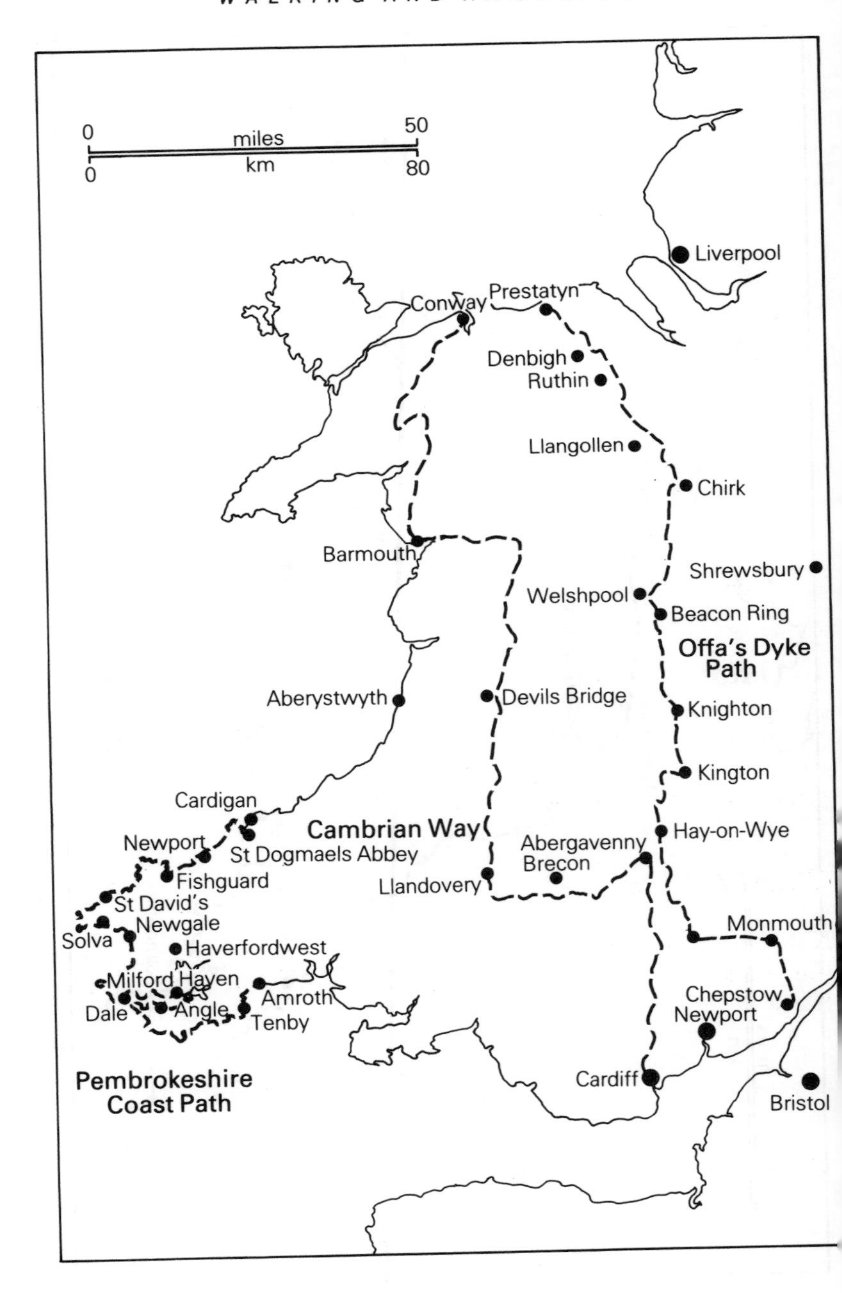
0
miles
50
0
km
80
Liverpool
Conway
Prestatyn
Denbigh
Ruthin
Llangollen
Chirk
Barmouth
Shrewsbury
Welshpool
Beacon Ring
Offa's Dyke Path
Aberystwyth
Devils Bridge
Knighton
Kington
Cardigan
Cambrian Way
Hay-on-Wye
Newport
St Dogmaels Abbey
Abergavenny
Brecon
Fishguard
Llandovery
St David's
Newgale
Solva
Monmouth
Haverfordwest
Milford Haven
Amroth
Chepstow
Dale
Angle
Tenby
Newport
Cardiff
Bristol
Pembrokeshire Coast Path

Circular routes

Not all of the paths are linear. There are now circular routes in many parts of the country. There are named walks round many of our cities and counties, which enable you to complete a circular route in small stages. These have the advantage of providing a long route over a variety of countryside without moving too far from your base.

The **Leicestershire Round**, for instance, gives you 100 miles (161km) through the most beautiful and historical parts of the county, cutting through all the radial roads out of Leicester, which provide you with bus routes back into the city, or out into the neighbouring little market towns, so that the whole walk can be done using public transport and you can sleep in your own bed, or in your tent or in a local farmhouse or inn.

There are walks like the **Leeds Country Way**, which circles 60 miles (97km) around Leeds and the **Sheffield Country Walk**, which provides 53 miles (85km). Even London has its own **London Countryway**, a 200-mile (322-km) circular path with surprisingly quiet beauty and steep hills!

Coastal footpaths

Various islands provide coastal footpaths: the Isle of Man has 90 miles (145km) of waymarked route; the Isle of Wight has a 60-mile (97-km) route; and there is one of 126 miles (203km) round Anglesey.

Short routes

Not all the named paths are particularly long! There are short waymarked routes like the 12-mile (20-km) **Knightley Way** in Northamptonshire, which can easily be done in a day. A strong walker could do it in both directions in one day. Lesser mortals can arrange transport for the return journey, or arrange to stop overnight at the Youth Hostel at Badby or a hotel at Greens Norton and walk it back next day.

Finding more information

Each LDP has an explanatory leaflet or guide which helps with addresses and advice about where to stay. Read the guide book and choose a stretch that is not too arduous, and remember that if the paths are linear, you are going to need to arrange transport at each end or come back the way you went or work out a circular route on unmarked paths!

Ask at your information office for details of your nearest named path. You may not have to travel far to reach an interesting, local long distance path. You can then decide whether to tackle it in one fell swoop, or in bits and bobs, sampling the easiest or most attractive parts.

These are choices you can make for yourself, using the information you pick up from walking magazines or guide books, from HMSO publications and from tourist offices or from other walkers. But remember that there is more to our highway system than motorways and there is a whole network of quieter and lesser known footpaths for you to choose to walk! You do not have to limit yourself to named routes and long distance paths. You can branch out and explore!

7.2 Areas of Outstanding Natural Beauty

Perhaps you want to explore a different part of the country during a long weekend break. The Countryside Commission has designated various Areas of Outstanding Natural Beauty where special efforts are made by the county council to keep unwanted development out and to retain the character of the landscape, its farming use and wildlife. These are excellent walking areas, with a network of footpaths and bridleways that provide easy access. You can either follow these or branch off on your own and plan a route.

White Peak

The southern half of the Peak District National Park, known as the White Peak because of its limestone composition, is dissected by deep valleys. Clear streams run through these valleys—or dales—and there are excellent footpaths for walkers. Buxton, Matlock and Ashbourne are all good points to explore from. Dovedale is probably the best known: from Thorpe Cloud up to Hartington is one of the finest walks in the country. The **Tissington Trail** from Mapleton to Hartington, mentioned earlier, is 11 miles (18km) of grass track with waymarked walks leading off it.

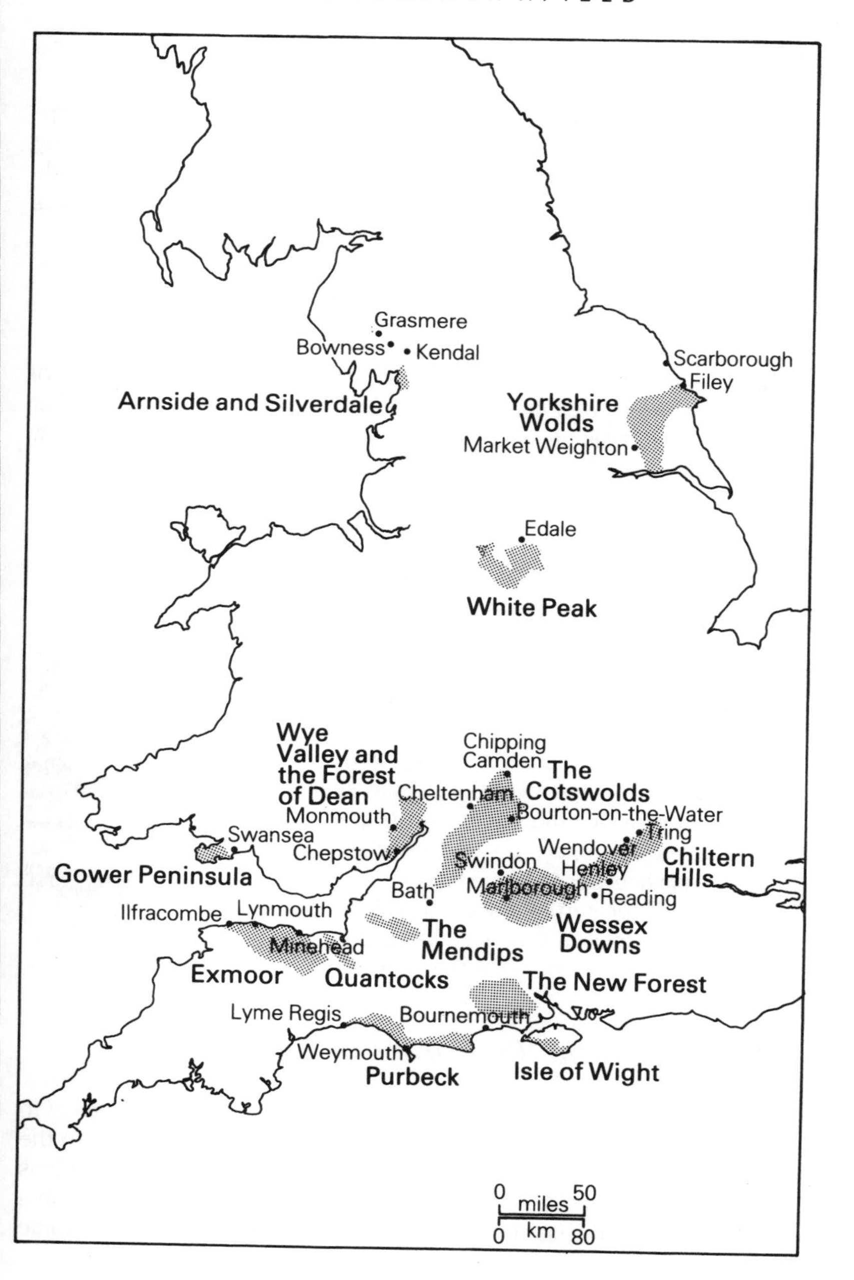
Grasmere
Bowness
Kendal
Arnside and Silverdale
Scarborough
Filey
Yorkshire Wolds
Market Weighton
Edale
White Peak
Wye Valley and the Forest of Dean
Chipping Camden
The Cotswolds
Cheltenham
Bourton-on-the-Water
Monmouth
Swansea
Chepstow
Tring
Wendover
Chiltern Hills
Gower Peninsula
Swindon
Henley
Bath
Marlborough
Reading
Ilfracombe
Lynmouth
The Mendips
Wessex Downs
Minehead
Exmoor
Quantocks
The New Forest
Lyme Regis
Bournemouth
Weymouth
Purbeck
Isle of Wight
0 miles 50
0 km 80

Yorkshire Wolds

Less challenging than the Yorkshire Moors, the Wolds are an escarpment of chalk hills overlooking the Vale of Pickering. This is farming country, with some of the prettiest dry dales of the area. Few roads penetrate, but there are plenty of waymarked paths. The **Wolds Way** is one of the easiest LDPs to follow.

Arnside and Silverdale

Walking in the Lake District is splendid, of course, if you like plenty of company! The less well-known Arnside and Silverdale areas nearby offer plenty of good walking on limestone hills—and the estuary and low marshy valleys are interesting to explore.

The Cotswolds

The Cotswold Hills are a high limestone escarpment looking over the Severn Vale. The **Cotswold Way** runs along the escarpment from Chipping Camden to Bath. The uplands are farming country dotted with neat stone walls and old hedgerows, and walking is mainly on the old farm tracks. The wolds were once vast sheepwalks which provided the wealth for the gracious town houses and churches of the area. The rivers are particularly lovely and their meanders link strings of little settlements. The villages and market towns, built in Cotswold limestone, are some of the most charming in the country.

Wye Valley and the Forest of Dean

The ancient Royal Forest of Dean is still richly wooded and it is easy to get lost in the maze of tracks and paths. It is a good idea to keep to the waymarked paths or the Forestry Commission's nature trails—unless you know you are an excellent map reader. The River Wye flows in a series of loops down to the Severn by Chepstow, and there are some good walks high above the river.

Gower Peninsula

An area of beautiful scenery and fine coastal walking, the Gower Peninsula is a wonderful place to escape to from the industrial valleys of South Wales.

Chiltern Hills

These chalk hills to the north-west of London have their own distinct character. Long ridges fall away southwards, with enchanting little villages in the valleys. There is a fine network of rural paths, all well signposted.

Wessex Downs

This is one of the finest chalk upland areas, and extends across Berkshire and Wiltshire into Hampshire. As you walk on the springy turf you will be following in ancient footsteps along prehistoric tracks and Roman roads—traces of ancient settlements are everywhere. The **Ridgeway Path**, mentioned earlier, provides fine walking past the Iron Age hill forts of Segsbury, Uffington, Liddington and Barbury, and past chambered barrows and the great stone Circle of Avebury. Marlborough is an ideal exploring centre.

The Mendips

The Mendips are a range of modest hills just south of Bristol. There are relatively few footpaths. But if you like walking on lanes there is a maze of those. On a fine weekend they can be crowded, but at other times you might find peace and solitude.

Exmoor and the Quantocks

Exmoor is less wild than Dartmoor, and more approachable for the less experienced walker. Paths are plentiful and well signposted, and there are a number of permissive paths, opened by the owners as a special concession. The Quantocks are a separate range of gently rounded and bracken-covered low hills. Together they comprise the best of North Devon and Somerset's walking country.

The New Forest

A mixture of wild open heathland and woodland in ancient enclosures, the New Forest offers plenty of easy walking, though it is easy to get lost! Careful mapreading is essential. You might come across the famous New Forest ponies, or herds of deer. Lyndhurst is a good centre to explore the area from.

Isle of Purbeck

This part of the Dorset coast (it is not an island!) provides both downland and coastal walks within a very small area. The ridge walk along the Purbeck Hills takes you to splendid Corfe Castle. A cliff path follows the finest unspoilt coastline in the south, including the lovely Lulworth Cove and the arch of Durdle Door.

Isle of Wight

This is excellent walking country for those who like variety. The **Tennyson Trail** from Carisbrooke to Alum Bay offers varied downland and forest walking, and fine marine views. The **Worsley Trail** from Shanklin Old Village to Brighstone Forest, covers forest, downland and high countryside. Or if you are feeling really energetic, the **Coastal Path** circles the whole 60-mile (97-km) coastline. However, the bus service on the Isle of Wight is very good, so it is a good area for planning your own route.

These are just some of the beautiful walking areas in this country. There are hundreds more—probably on your own doorstep. The choice is yours—to follow a well-trodden path in a popular tourist area, or to go off and explore and find new delights for yourself.

BIBLIOGRAPHY

When you see unusual things on a walk you often want to identify them. You don't need to carry all the reference books with you, if you learn to identify the main features or if you take photographs of what you see so that you can look them up later. But you could slip into your pocket a small reference book for the aspect which most interests you.

Your interest could lead you to the bigger reference books to answer more complicated questions. Evening classes might help you to find your way around the books or to understand the answers given by scholars, or to put your interest in a wider context.

Specialist groups, clubs or societies can often provide alternative answers and give you more practical experience. Lists of societies and classes are usually available from your library and information service or adult education centre.

Mountain and hill walking

If you wish to move on to higher things, read specialist books such as:

Langmuir, Eric *Mountaincraft and Leadership* (1984) Scottish Sports Council. (Trade distribution by Cordee, 3a de Montfort Street, Leics.) This tells you about mountain navigation and safety and such hazards as exposure and exhaustion.

Part 1

Wainwright, A. Various pictorial guides, Westmorland Gazette.
Wilson, John G. *Follow the Ordnance Survey Guide* (1985) Black.
HMSO Guides to various coastal and long distance paths.

Part 2

The complete article by Lucretia Clark is quoted in full in MacDermid, H. *The Well Trodden Path, the story of one hundred years' of footpath preservation in Leicestershire* (1987) trade distribution by Cordee.

Part 4

Clayden, Paul & Trevelyan, John *Rights of Way: A Guide to Law and Practice* (1983) Open Spaces Society and Ramblers Association.
A most useful reference book with a good index.

Books about the history of the landscape

Hoskins, W. *The Making of the English Landscape* ed. C. Taylor (1988) Hodder and Stoughton.

Muir, Richard *The Shell Guide to Reading the Landscape* (1984) Michael Joseph.
Beresford, M. *History on the Ground* (1957) Lutterworth Press.

The history of roads and tracks

Taylor, Christopher *The Roads and Tracks of Britain* (1979) Dent.
Hindle, B. P. *Medieval Roads* (1989) Shire Publications.
Addison, W. *Old Roads of England* (1980) Batsford.
Watkins, Alfred *The Old Straight Track* (1925) Methuen; (1974) London Abacus.
It is full of interesting observations; but ignore the theories about ley lines, etc. To be taken with a (large) pinch of salt!

Part 6

Nature Books

Choose a really good expensive one for reference or a little one to take with you, for example:
Hamlyn Guide to Birds of Britain
Observer's Book of Trees
Mabey, Richard *Food for Free* (1989) Collins.
Jordan, Michael *Mushroom Magic* (1989) Elm Tree Books.

Place names

Ekwall, E. *The Concise Oxford Dictionary of Place Names* (1974) Oxford University Press.
Gelling, Margaret *Signposts to the Past* (1978) Dent.

Old travellers' records

Leland, John *Itinerary 1546*
The Journeys of Celia Fiennes 1685–1703
Defoe, Daniel *A Tour through the whole Island of Great Britain 1724–6*

Part 7

Long distance paths

The Long Distance Paths Advisory Service keeps an up-to-date record of all new LDPs. *The Long Distance Walkers Handbook* by Barbara Blatchford (Black, 1991) gives a good guide to the most popular and well known. There are leaflets and guide books to these and many more, available from information centres, book shops and libraries.

Wainwright, A. *On the Pennine Way* (1985) Michael Joseph.
Andrew, Ken *The Southern Upland Way* (1984) HMSO Official Guide.

Useful Addresses

Holiday organisations

Camping and Caravanning Club
Greenfields House
Westwood Way
Coventry
West Midlands CV4 8JH
Tel: 0203 694995

Holiday Fellowship
HF Holidays Ltd
Imperial House
Edgware Road
Colindale
London NW9 5AL
Tel: 081-905 9558

Rambler's Association
1/5 Wandsworth Road
London SW8 2XX
Tel: 071-582 6878
(The Yearbook contains an accommodation guide and a section of useful addresses.)

Youth Hostels Association
Trevelyan House
8 St Stephen's Hill
St Albans
Herts AL1 2DY
Tel: 0727 45047

Organisations concerned with the countryside

Council for the Protection of Rural England (CPRE)
4 Hobart Place
London SW1W 0HY
Tel: 071-235 9481

Council for the Protection of Rural Wales (CPRW)
Ty Gwyn
31 High Street
Welshpool
Powys SY21 7JP
Tel: 0938 2525

Countryside Commission
John Dower House
Crescent Place
Cheltenham
Gloucestershire GL50 3RA
Tel: 0242 521381

Countryside Commission for Scotland
Battleby House
Redgorton
Perth PH1 3EW
Tel: 0738 27921

Forestry Commission
231 Corstorphine Road
Edinburgh EH12 7AT
Tel: 031-334 0303

National Trust
36 Queen Anne's Gate
London SW1H 9AS
Tel: 071-222 9251

National Trust for Scotland
5 Charlotte Square
Edinburgh EH2 4DU
Tel: 031-226 5922

Nature Conservancy Council
Northminster House
Peterborough PE1 1UA
Tel: 0733 40345

Organisations concerned with paths and rights of way

Backpackers' Club
PO Box 381
7–10 Friar Street
Reading RG3 4RL
Tel: 04917 739

Byways and Bridleways Trust
9 Queen Anne's Gate
London SW1H 9BY

Long Distance Paths Advisory Service
The Barn
Holm Lyon
Burnside
Kendal
Cumbria LA9 6QX
Tel: 0539 27837

Long Distance Walkers Association
Hon Sec: Alan Castle
Wayfarers
9 Tainters Brook
Uckfield
East Sussex TN22 1UQ

Regional tourist boards

Cumbria Tourist Board
Ashleigh
Holly Road
Windermere
Cumbria LA23 2AQ
Tel: 096 62 4444

East Anglia Tourist Board
Toppesfield Hall
Hadleigh
Suffolk IP7 5DN
Tel: 0473 822922

East Midlands Tourist Board
Exchequergate
Lincoln LN2 1PZ
Tel: 0522 531521

Heart of England Tourist Board
Woodside
Larkhill
Worcester WR5 2EF
Tel: 0905 763436

London Tourist Board
26 Grosvenor Gardens
London SW1W 0DU
Tel: 071-730 3450

North West Tourist Board
The Last Drop Village
Bromley Cross
Bolton
Lancashire BL7 9PZ
Tel: 0204 591511

Northumbria Tourist Board
Aykley Heads
Durham DH1 5UX
Tel: 091 384 6905

South East England Tourist Board
The Old Brew House
Warwick Park
Tunbridge Wells
Kent TN2 5TA
Tel: 0892 540766

Southern Tourist Board
40 Chamberlayne Road
Eastleigh
Hampshire SO5 5JH
Tel: 0703 620006

Thames & Chilterns Tourist Board
The Mount House
Church Green
Witney
Oxfordshire OX8 6DZ
Tel: 0993 778800

West Country Tourist Board
Trinity Court
27 Southernhay East
Exeter EX1 1QS
Tel: 0392 76351

Yorkshire & Humberside Tourist Board
312 Tadcaster Road
York YO2 2HF
Tel: 0904 707961

INDEX

MORE BOOKS FROM TEACH YOURSELF

CANOEING

RAY ROWE

Ray Rowe has written a practical introduction to canoeing and kayaking that will have you hooked. This highly illustrated book contains:

* descriptions of the different kinds of boats
* guidance on how to choose a boat that suits you
* advice on what other equipment you need
* step-by-step guides to basic techniques and boat control; rescue, including the eskimo roll; white water techniques
* hints on flat water paddling, canoe touring and camping
* hints on sea touring

Teach Yourself Canoeing will give you information and the techniques you need to get you started with confidence.

TEACH YOURSELF

FLOWER ARRANGING

JUDITH BLACKLOCK

Flower arranging is easy. You don't need to have artistic talent, a large garden or plenty of spare time – all you need are a few basics and the guidance contained within this book.

Teach Yourself Flower Arranging is for the complete beginner. Early chapters introduce the different elements – foliage, the flowers themselves, equipment – with helpful suggestions as to how they can be obtained without spending a fortune. Whether you want to create a simple bowl of flowers for the home, a gift for a friend or an arrangement for a special occasion, the easy, step-by-step instructions and full illustrations will enable you to create the effect you desire. Once you have mastered the basic shapes you may find that you want to experiment with ideas of your own and Judith Blacklock is ready with a variety of designs to stir your imagination.

With invaluable advice on choosing plant material, preserving the life of your arrangement, wild flowers and growing your own foliage and flowers, this book provides an original and hugely enjoyable introduction to this ever-popular art.

TEACH YOURSELF

GOLF

BERNARD GALLACHER AND MARK WILSON

Including the complete Rules of Golf

All golfers, from junior novice to superstar professional, are united by one indisputable attraction: there is no end to the process of learning to play the game. *Teach Yourself Golf* has been written and illustrated to meet the needs of golfers of all standards. It covers every department of the game, from choosing a set of clubs to detailed advice on how to play the trouble shots that win competitions. The language of golf for those who play and those who follow the game through televised tournaments is explained in a comprehensive glossary. Whatever your handicap or experience, this book will help you learn, improve and enjoy the game more than ever.

'A book which could make a big impact for the beginner and the novice.' *Golf Illustrated*

TEACH YOURSELF